The Incomplete Guide
to the Art of Discovery

The Incomplete Guide
to the Art of Discovery

JACK E. OLIVER

Columbia University Press
New York

Columbia University Press

New York   Oxford

Library of Congress Cataloging-in-Publication Data

Oliver, J. E. (Jack Ertle)
  The incomplete guide to the art of discovery / Jack E. Oliver.
    p.   cm.
  Includes bibliographical references and index.
  ISBN 0-231-07620-7—ISBN 0-231-07621-5 (pbk.)
  1. Research.   2. Research—Methodology.   I. Title.
Q180.A1044   1991
507.2—dc20   91-16635
                                                                CIP

Casebound editions of Columbia University Press
books are Smyth-sewn and printed on permanent and
durable acid-free paper.

Printed in the United States of America

c 10 9 8 7 6 5 4 3 2 1

p 10 9 8 7 6 5 4 3 2 1

Contents

PREFACE ix

1. About Discovery 1
Purpose and Scope 2
The Joy of Discovery 7
Importance to Society 8
An Art and a Science 9
Intended Audience 11
The Organization of What Follows 12
A Little Background in Earth Science 13

2. Strategy for Discovery 31
Don't Follow the Crowd 32
Rebel, but Wisely 35
Strive to Enhance Serendipity 37
Avoid Science Eddies 39
Study the Earth, *and* the Science of Geology 41
Seek the Nonquestions 43
See Your Era in Long-Term Perspective 46
Go with Intuition 48
Avoid Sidetracking to Trivia 52

Be Competitive, Be a Winner, Be First   54
Argue by Analogy   57
Vision, Hypotheses, and Objective Testing   59
The Strategy of Exploration for Understanding   62

3. Tactics for Discovery   66
Adapt and Adopt Instruments and Techniques   66
Skim the Cream   69
Minimize Jargon   71
Speak (Listen) to the Earth, and It Shall Teach Thee   72
Go for the Spatial Pattern   78
How to Choose a Graduate School   81
Skim the Rest of the Volume, Any Volume   84
Do It Yourself   86
The Knack of the Fresh Perspective   87
Choose Your Problem Very Carefully   89
The Curve of Discovery   92
Overcoming the "Terminal" Paper   93

4. Personal Traits and Attitudes for Discoverers   97
Never Confuse Sophistication with Understanding   98
Enjoy the Struggle, Not the Spoils   100
Never Fully Accept Any Hypothesis, Theory, Law, or
Doctrine   103
Respect, Not Reverence   105
Let's Hear It for Enthusiasm   108
There Is No Limit to What You Can Accomplish if Someone
Else Gets the Credit   110
Humility Leads to Discovery   110
Audacity Leads to Discovery   113
Be Optimistic, at Least Secretly   115
Avoid All Pretense   116
Remember a Scientist's Debt to Society   118
Dream a Little, or a Lot   121
Occasionally, Think Like a Child   122
Work Hard, Then Harder   124
Some Characteristics of an Innovator   125

5. Caveats   127

Beware of Indoctrination   127

Beware of Occam's Razor   129

Beware of Classification Schemes   133

6. A Few Views and Comments on Science   136

How, Not Why   137

A Science Among the Sciences   139

Will Science Stifle Itself?   143

The Discoverers and the Do-It-Righters   146

Big Science Vs. Little Science, The Wrong Focus   149

The Fundamental Conflict Between Bureaucracy and
Science   152

The Joy and the Perils of Success   155

Youth and Age   156

There Is Only One Earth   159

How to Recognize an Important Contribution to Science   160

How to Recognize That You Have Made an Important
Discovery   163

Major Discoveries Are Not Made Democratically   164

7. The Inside Story of One Discovery   167

8. Closing Remarks   187

POSTSCRIPT   193

REFERENCES   197

INDEX   199

Preface

DURING my career in science, now nearly a half century in duration, I have grown more and more aware that success in science, paralleling success in most careers, comes not so much to the most gifted, nor the most skillful, nor the most knowledgeable, nor the most affluent of scientists, but rather to the superior strategist and tactician. The individual who is able to maneuver with propriety through the world of science along a course that regularly puts him or her in a position of serendipity is often the one who excels. Consequently, I have long sought to observe the experiences and the personal styles of successful scientists and to identify common traits that might be acquired and used profitably by others as they direct their careers. This book is a summary of those observations and hence can serve as a guide to the ambitious young scientist or student of science.

However, no matter how well we prepare and plan, no matter how carefully we make our decisions and guide our actions, fate still seems always to play a central role in our careers and our lives. Often an apparently insignificant incident turns out to be a critical step to important developments that follow. In this preface, I relate the chain of incidents that led me to the gateway of the world of discovery and hence ultimately to the writing of this book. In so doing I hope not only to set the stage for what follows but also to set an appropriate tone of caution for a book that purports, somewhat optimistically, to be a guide in a subject that is never fully predictable.

In the fall of 1946, Columbia played Yale in the Yale Bowl. During the post–World War II years, the stature and caliber of Ivy League football was unusually high as war veterans returned to school and reinforced the normal complement of younger athletes. Stadia were filled; tickets were scalped; Ivy League teams made headlines. The contest in New Haven was a particularly exciting one. Yale dominated early play and led at the half by two touchdowns, but Columbia rallied to pull ahead late in the game and win. For me that game was especially memorable. In the last quarter, I was able to block a Yale punt and so set up the winning score for Columbia. It was a notable event in an athletic career that was otherwise largely undistinguished. Long forgotten by others, that moment of success will stand out in my memory for life.

But strangely that unusual achievement was not the most important thing that happened to me during that game. An obscure event earlier began an unlikely chain of happenings that had a far more profound effect on my life. The event set me onto the trail of discovery in science and eventually onto the writing of this book. Surely unnoticed by spectators, and inconsequential with regard to the outcome of the contest, the event was a key incident in the development of my career and my life. While blocking on one play, which as I recall was a routine plunge into the line for little gain, I foolishly put my outstretched hand on the turf. An opposing player promptly stepped on it—with his cleats, of course. The injury that resulted was not crippling, but it did require frequent application of liniment and bandage during the following week or so. The liniment was the critical element in what followed.

At the time, I was taking an intermediate-level course in electricity and magnetism. It was given by Professor Polykarp Kusch, later a Nobel laureate in physics. The course was designed for, and populated by, physics majors, of which I was one. Now it often happens that members of a particular subset of society develop a common social attitude toward certain matters outside the mutual interest that defines the subset. In this manner, physicists and physics students of that era were conditioned to downplay or ignore athletics. They wanted to be like Oppenheimer, not Dimaggio, or Davis and Blanchard, or Sugar Ray Robinson. Modern physicists are often sports minded and sports conscious, but they were much less so then. Consequently, no one in that physics class knew that I was an athlete, nor did I in turn know whether any of the other students were athletes.

The liniment quickly changed that. The strong aroma that accompanied me as I entered the classroom was detected by all and immediately identified by one, a wrestler named Dick Edwards. Dick knew that the familiar odor came from the Columbia trainer's private concoction and immediately deduced that another varsity athlete was in the class. He sniffed me out and struck up a conversation. The camaraderie of athletes prevailed and we became friends. Without the liniment, we might never have become acquainted in the no-nonsense environment of that course. Dick, it turned out, would arrange my introduction to geophysics.

At the end of the academic year, I made a late decision to forego my senior year of college in order to begin graduate study in physics at Columbia during the following semester. It was a sound decision academically but not financially. Life as a graduate student was more expensive than I had anticipated. Early in the fall of 1947, I confided to a friend that I needed money and was seeking a job. As luck would have it, the conversation was overheard by Dick Edwards, and he kindly volunteered some help. Dick led me to an unfamiliar part of the campus and introduced me to his employer, Professor Maurice Ewing. In less than five minutes Ewing interviewed me, offered me a job, and I accepted with delight. As I left Ewing's office, I noticed the title "Professor of Geology" on the door. It struck me that he must have thought that I was a graduate student in geology, not physics. I reentered his office and said, "Professor Ewing, I'd like that job very much. However, you're a professor of geology. You didn't ask me about it, but I feel I must point out that I've never studied geology in my life." I was certain he would withdraw the offer and I would once again be job seeking.

Instead Ewing's response was my introduction to the real world of science, a world that extends far beyond the strict organization and regimentation of classrooms, curricula, and textbooks. "Well," he said, smiling and shaking my hand, "that'll be two of us!" Ewing would become one of the greatest of earth scientists, and of course, he knew a great deal of geology, but it was all self-taught or learned informally from others. His Ph.D. was in physics and he never studied geology in a formal way.

That incident was an eye-opener and a confidence-builder for me. I began to recognize that the order, convention, routine, and organization that characterize one's early indoctrination into science do not prevail at higher levels. Ewing's lively reassurance was a breath of fresh air for a plodding student. As all scientists know, scientific research is much more a series of independent or loosely coordinated individual attacks on the unknown than an orchestrated advance by platoons of identical scientist-soldiers. And the life of a scientist is more appealing and challenging as a result. Ewing conveyed that message with a smile, a handshake, and a few words.

The effects of that job went well beyond the opening incident. As I worked with Ewing and his group, I quickly became aware of, and enamored by, study of the earth. Ewing introduced his students to the joy of discovery, to the great range of opportunity for discovery, and to the challenge of exploring the earth. Before long I was flying balloons in New Mexico, sailing the Atlantic and becoming seasick on a research vessel, and exploring the frigid ice pack of the Arctic Ocean. And my new colleagues formed an enthusiastic, inspiring, and congenial group. I soon reoriented my ambitions and became his student. Ewing's style of science with its broad scope, earthly and outdoor orientation, demanding nature, touch of adventure, and seemingly endless opportunity for discovery captivated me for life. I have never turned back.

What follows in this book is by no means based solely on experiences with one program, nor is it exclusively an exposition of Ewing's or any other one scientist's style. I have been influenced by many scientists, students of science, and stories of scientific discovery. But the following does reflect the fascination for discovery that was kindled by the fateful events of the liniment, the friend, and the great professor, and I try here to pass it on to others so inclined. The effort of writing this book will be fully rewarded if only a single reader is caught up in the enchantment of discovery, even more so if that indoctrination can be achieved without destructive application of cleats of a football shoe!

In another vein, I note that to bring the ideas of this book to a broad and unknown audience leaves me with a feeling of apprehension and uneasiness. I am apprehensive because some of the ideas are surely controversial and to be challenged by others. I am uneasy because every scientist's efforts, no matter how independent the work or writing, are a product of innumerable associatiions with others, most of whom cannot be fully credited in a work in which only a limited number of names can appear. With full knowledge that a simple statement is inadequate, I would nevertheless like to acknoweldge and thank all those who have helped me, knowingly or unknowingly, along the way.

I would also like to acknowledge with gratitude the organizations that have made my career, and hence this book, possible. I have been fortunate to hold faculty positions at two great universities, Columbia and Cornell, each of which gave me the freedom and encouragement to pursue discovery and the stature to make something happen. In addition, I have received financial support for research from various private organizations, foundations, and companies and from numerous government agencies, including particularly the National Science Foundation, the Air Force Office of Scientific Research, the Office of Naval Research, and NASA.

Various reviewers, colleagues, and students, especially Bryan Isacks, Robert Litak, and Raymond Culotta, read drafts of the book and made helpful comments. Judy Healey and Kathleen Vargason prepared the manuscript and patiently made seemingly endless revisions.

Finally, I would like to dedicate this effort to my three honeys, wife Gay and daughters Nelly and Amy.

The Incomplete Guide
to the Art of Discovery

O N E

About Discovery

D<small>ISCOVERY</small>, n.: The finding of something previously un-known." DISCOVERY! THE STUFF OF NEWSPAPER HEAD-LINES AND PRIME-TIME TV! Discovery: A phenomenon at the core of that part of the human spirit that strives continually to unravel the unknown and so improve the lot of humans. *Discovery:* an agreeable word often found in the company of other pleasant yet mind-jogging terms such as *exciting, stimulating, satisfying, astonishing,* and *rewarding.* Discovery; A process familiar to all humans because, at one time or another, they have all discovered.

As the foregoing implies, discovery is a widespread, multifaceted phenomenon. Sometimes it is of immense importance, sometimes it is of trivial consequence. Strangely, although discoveries themselves are often the subject of much attention, the process of discovery is rarely examined explicitly by practicing scientists. What is it that we think or do in order to produce discovery? Perhaps the subject receives little attention because discovery is ubiquitous and diverse and because the many styles of discovery are so different. One could hardly hope to examine the phenomenon of discovery in all its many modes and do so comprehensively.

In the following pages I have set down some selected aspects of the discovery process under conditions and constraints outlined in the next few sections. The treatment is not complete; it could never be, for discovery itself is not, and can never be, complete. Nevertheless, discovery is a human activity so fascinating and so important that an incomplete and imperfect attempt to understand and stimulate it may well be worthwhile.

The remaining sections of this introductory chapter set the tone and outline the bounds for the attempt that follows.

Purpose and Scope

THIS is a book about science. It is not, however, a conventional, middle-of-the-road, bread-and-butter, scientific book. It is not about scientific data, or scientific hypotheses, or scientific conclusions. It is not even a product of the scientific method. But it is about a matter that should be of interest to scientists and others who seek to develop their capacity to innovate, to create, or to discover.

This book is about the subjective process that accompanies discovery. It is about how to choose a discovery-laden topic for research, how to find opportunities in science overlooked by others, and, particularly, how to break out of the rut of mundane thinking that traps most of us most of the time.

Or at least that is what I would like this book to be about. Perhaps it is, perhaps it is not. The subject is one that defies mastery or even control. By its very nature, discovery is inseparable from the unknown. And any attempt to chart a course to or through the unknown is chancy at best. There is no universal recipe for discovery. There is no guaranteed route to discovery. The scientist who seeks to discover must follow a course that cannot be fully defined or anticipated. That is the dilemma of this subject and why the subject is often bypassed.

However, the existence of the dilemma does not mean that the subject should be ignored. Far from it. We live in the age of science, one of the most fertile periods for intellectual advance in all of history. Major discoveries occur often in modern science, minor discoveries still more frequently. With the process of discovery so readily available for observation, it should be possible for us to learn how to modify our activities and our behavior so as to improve our opportunities for discovery in the future. We cannot guarantee discovery, but we can influence serendipity by learning from, adhering to, and building on, patterns of prior success.

The chief purpose of this book, then, is to enhance serendipity in those who aspire to discovery. To some this goal will seem beyond reach and the thought of reaching for it presumptuous. Discovery, the revealing of something unknown, is by nature fraught with surprise. Serendipity, that special and happy knack for finding valuable or agreeable things not sought, often seems more an inborn gift or divine blessing than a characteristic that can be built into humans like the muscles of a weight lifter.

Nevertheless, it seems that, to a degree, serendipity can be acquired. Surely there must be ways for an individual to proceed in order to become more "happy-accident prone." Skeptics should note that it is certainly feasible to develop effective guidelines for one who seeks to become "unhappy-accident prone." The converse must also be true.

The way to enhancement of serendipity is to observe the process of discovery by others and to recognize patterns of behavior and activity that, while not guaranteeing discovery, can nevertheless improve one's chances for discovery significantly. The theme of this book may thus be stated simply. *To discover, act like a discoverer.*

The task of mapping and following the patterns of previous discovery is not straightforward. The recorded history of past discovery is spotty at best and only rarely provides an accurate and thorough account of the information critical to our objective. Historians tend to provide a record of key events of the past, all fit together in a logical sequence that is apparent in the historical perspective. But to learn how to discover, we want to know about the subjective decision making, the role of insight and intuition, and the scientist's perception of the work while it was going on, not just someone else's view of the result after it took its place in a historical sequence of events. We want to know how and why the scientist thought and acted as he or she did, what parts of previous experience and training bore on the discovery, and how interaction with others aided or hindered the discovery process.

Occasionally an author, perhaps the discoverer or a colleague or a biographer, records such information in biographical style, but most goes unrecorded. Certainly the "inside story" of how a discovery was made does not appear in modern scientific journals. For such journals, and perhaps more because of convention than conviction, great pains are taken to ensure that the subjective side of science is not included as a part of the formal scientific record.

Nevertheless, most scientists have personal experience with discoveries of their own, or of colleagues, and so can piece together the unspoken and unrecorded ingredients that led to discovery. Such experience is implicitly a basis for the evolving style of that scientist.

Of course, there remains the very real and very important possibility of great discovery in the future by someone following a completely unprecedented path or style. We must keep our minds open for such an achievement and such a new route to success. But by definition, a major revelation of such nature is not something we can have much hope of planning for, and hence, this book is directed elsewhere, toward the abundant yet important discovery that takes place in more common, but not always well-recognized or well-recorded, style.

To a degree, this book is about both discovery and discovery's partner, innovation. Those two topics are not strictly the same, but they share a common basis that encourages discussion of them jointly. Innovation, the art of introducing something new, goes hand in hand with discovery, the art of revealing something previously unknown. Both involve the precious element of creativity. Those with a knack for one are likely to be adept at the other.

What follows is based largely on my experience with discovery and discoverers. My career has spanned, and so I have been fortunate to observe, a period of major discovery in my field, solid earth science. Sometimes that discovery has taken place in the building where I worked, sometimes partway around the world. All such discovery is, however, linked together in the flow of the science during this period, so I have been able to sense it all to some degree. Heavy reliance on personal experience limits the scope and generality of the book, of course, and invites comment and criticism from those with a different set of experiences. That is fair enough. Most such criticism will likely be to the good, and if a constructive interplay develops, a purpose of the book will have been served.

The book is not simply a collection of stories of past achievements. Instead, I have tried to organize and generalize the lessons of various experiences so as to produce a set of guidelines for the discovery-bound scientist. The basis for the guidelines is thus broader than the examples of the text. Collectively the guidelines are an attempt to lay out favorable routes to discovery. The guidelines are not, however, highly ordered or interconnected. Most of them stand alone and can be read independently of the surrounding text. Furthermore, the guidelines appear with headings that occasionally seem to play loose with the profundity of science. They take the form of slogans or mottoes, or even locker room posters. This book is about serious matters, but it is not a sepulchral tome. It is written in conversational style. And there is an obvious strain of encouragement in it. One might call it cheerleading. That is intentional. Modern science is a fascinating world full of exciting and enjoyable opportunities. There is no room or reason for a scientist who lacks zest or who aspires to mediocrity. A scientist should have lofty goals. Encouragement is as appropriate for young scientists as for anyone in any field, and this book tries to do its share.

Examples, stories, and histories are mostly, though not entirely, taken from some aspect of earth science. There are two reasons for this orientation. One is that the author is a geophysicist with the bulk of his experience in earth science. The other is that solid earth science, with the discovery of plate tectonics, underwent a major revolution during the 1960s. Thus scientists who began their careers at or near the time of World War II have been privileged to observe (1) the preplate tectonics era when the science lacked a globally unifying concept and was highly fragmented; (2) the coming of the plate tectonics concept, the story of earth's spreading seas and colliding continents, that brought the science together; and (3) the succeeding era when plate tectonics reigns as the paradigm, and puzzle-solving science, in

Kuhn's terminology, prevails. A rich and varied spectrum of discovery from these eras is thus available for citation. Furthermore, the great advance in earth science that is plate tectonics is rather widely known and understood throughout science, so the examples have a base in the familiar for most scientists.

The emphasis on examples from earth science should not detract from the interest of students in other fields. Not all sciences are the same, of course. Some are very similar to earth science. Others differ markedly, usually because they are not so heavily observation oriented as earth science. Nevertheless, many of the guidelines should be applicable almost anywhere in science, and the examples likely have uncited counterparts in other fields of science as well. A later section provides a briefing on earth science and particularly the coming of plate tectonics for those who wish to become acquainted with, or refreshed in, this subject.

There is not much in this book about how to "do" science. There is, for example, little about how to set up a laboratory, or design an instrument, or devise a theory, or make an observation. Instead the book is about how to think and act in a way conducive to discovery and about how to develop an attitude that permits one to develop, accentuate, and capitalize on opportunities.

The next section describes a critical relation between human emotion and discovery.

The Joy of Discovery

FOR individuals born to the challenge of understanding nature, discovery is far more than a means to livelihood, far more than a spice of life. Discovery is the ultimate of human achievement. Discovery is thrill, excitement, and euphoria. Discovery is the difference between victory and defeat, between satisfaction and disappointment, between success and failure. Discovery is the prime goal of every true research scientist, every explorer of the great unknown. And commonly that quest for the pure joy of discovery is the prime motivation for their careers.

There are, of course, aspects of discovery much less agreeable than the sweet taste of success. Discovery may be fickle and unpredictable to the point of exasperation and frustration. It may be elusive to the point of dismay or the destruction of a career. It may be addictive to the point of dereliction of duty. Discovery may be two faced, sometimes producing surprise as the unknown is revealed, sometimes producing surprise that, after the utmost individual effort, the unknown is not revealed. Few scientists complete their careers without making a discovery of some sort, yet few make discoveries of major significance. And all scientists struggle through prolonged intervals of absence of discovery and the accompanying anxiety about a future that threatens to be discovery free.

Nevertheless, the star of discovery continues to shine brightly and to mesmerize those caught up in the challenge of exploring the unknown. That discovery is the ultimate goal is widely recognized by scientists, all of whom readily understand and make allowances for unconventional (though not unethical) behavior on the part of other scientists in the quest for discovery.

What makes discovery precious is not so much that discovery brings recognition, or honor, or advancement in a career. It is instead the unparalleled, private joy that comes from being the first human in all of history to acquire some particular piece of knowledge. The attraction of the joy of discovery is often overwhelming, but it is not the only motivation for the pursuit of discovery as I shall discuss in the next section.

Importance to Society

SOME scientists, like mountain climbers, seek their goal "because it's there." It is easy to understand and justify this approach to science. One cannot fault those who act on this motive.

But the process of scientific discovery is no longer, if indeed it ever was, a quest solely for the gratification of the individual scientist. In the modern world, and on our ever more densely populated earth with its ever more technologically dependent society, science has come to play a vital role in the progress of society. Continuing discovery is now essential to our welfare. We cannot hope to accommodate and support additional billions of humans on earth in the absence of increasing understanding of our environs and how we use and interact with them. Technology based on science is an indispensable component of modern society.

Of course, not all new science has immediate practical value. And a particular discovery may have positive or negative effects depending upon the way in which it is used by society. In the long run, however, and certainly in a collective sense, scientific discovery is beneficial, and society prospers as a result of the practical benefits of advances in science and technology.

Society as a whole also grows intellectually as a consequence of new perspectives and new understanding from scientific discovery. The view of earth from the moon, the panorama of the sea floor with its hidden mountain ranges and its deep trenches, and the story of the continental collisions that built our scenic and spectacular mountains have surely enriched our lives by stretching our horizons and by revealing the beauty and resolving the mysteries of the once unknown.

Because of science's generally positive effect, society has recognized and supported science and scientists. Scientists of the modern era are specially privileged. We are highly educated, often at the expense of the public. We have freedom to choose what activities we pursue, and often we are handsomely funded in such activities. We are supported to travel throughout the world in order to communicate with fellow scientists and so foster science. We are respected advisers and sources of authoritative views. With such privilege goes the enormous responsibility of conducting the scientific enterprise so as to provide maximum benefit to society. But just how to do so is never fully clear. There is no obvious optimum track or natural pace for science. Yet whether a particular scientific discovery is made now, or thirty years from now, may seriously affect the lives of millions, or billions, of humans. The awesome potential for affecting all of human existence provides the justification necessary for vigorous efforts to enhance the scientific enterprise in general and in particular to examine and improve the process of discovery. It is in this spirit that this book is written.

An Art and a Science

"IT'S an art, not a science!" Scientists cringe when they hear that expression. It is intended to draw a distinction between one type of activity (called an art), which is rooted in qualities such as skill, taste, style, and judgment, and a different kind of activity (called a science), which is supposedly methodical and structured to the point of nearly mechanical behavior by its practitioners. Scientists dislike the expression because the distinction between these two types of endeavor is far less clear-cut than the expression implies.

There is, of course, a distinction. Science has an encompassing structure and formalism that is largely absent in art. But science also has a component that involves many of those qualities central to an art. Style, creativity, and virtuosity, for example, are crucial in science, as they are in art. In fact, to make a major advance in science, an innovative style and a clever strategy may be critical ingredients. The scientist most skilled in those matters may well become the foremost discoverer.

It is correct, of course, that science builds a complex, interlocking structure of knowledge and that any new contribution to that structure must withstand rigorous, objective testing against other components of the structure. And all of the structure, new or old, is continually tested and retested against observation. Such testing and evaluation are not art; they are, in fact, what distinguishes science from art.

But, just how a scientist should go about selecting an entry to, and a place in, that structure; how the scientist should use his or her talents and efforts to make that contribution; and how the scientist should choose a subject that will lead to a significant, as opposed to a trivial, new contribution, are all matters to be decided in subjective fashion. In other words, designing the route to outstanding science *is* an art, in the sense that the term is used in the opening sentence of this section.

This book is about the side of science that is art in this sense, particularly the part that is here termed "the art of discovery." Proficiency in the art of discovery is at least as important to the scientist as is skill in the techniques of the science. Yet most formal education is limited to the techniques and the basic structure of science. The side that is art is normally given little explicit attention in the formal educational process. Often it is left as something to be born with or to be acquired through personal association with experienced practitioners of the art. Perhaps the latter process can be helped along by assembling some of the possible consequences of such an apprenticeship in printed form.

Intended Audience

THIS book is, of course, for anyone who cares to read it. But, in writing it, I have had in mind both a primary and a secondary audience. In the former category are students of science, particularly undergraduates or high school students with a distinct interest in science, graduate students seeking advanced degrees, and young scientists aspiring to improve their capacity for discovery. Like most professors with many years of campus experience, I have been delighted by the student who arrives with both the zeal and the talent to capitalize on major opportunities in science, and I have been distressed by the student who has comparable talent but who lacks that same zeal or aspiration. This book is partly the result of years of trying to implant that zeal and to heighten the aspirations of such students.

Laypeople or scholars with an interest in the scientific process are the secondary audience. Many of the guidelines for strategy, tactics, and personal attitudes described here apply equally well throughout science, many also to other facets of life. The need for innovation is ubiquitous, and the qualities that lead to innovation are always in demand. Those with little familiarity with science may be surprised by the emphasis on the importance of subjectivity in the scientific process. Scientists, of course, will not.

This book may be of interest to, but is not intended to reorient, seasoned discoverers, each of whom already has a formula for success. Likely that formula will in part differ and in part agree with the guidelines presented here, for there is no one successful style in science. And it is fortunate that there is not. Diversity of style is a marvelous asset that must be maintained in the research enterprise in order to ensure that no opportunity is missed. It would be highly detrimental to science if, suddenly, all scientists began to follow the same style. The goal of this book is to help someone, somewhere break out of the rut of routine activity and into the realm where discovery may be achieved. It is by no means intended to homogenize the science by encouraging all to adopt the same style and the same routes to discovery.

The Organization of What Follows

ALTHOUGH this volume is based on the subjective experiences of scientists with discovery, it is not biographical. Instead it lists and elaborates a number of guidelines that involve characteristics, principles, and procedures that seem conducive to discovery. The guidelines are organized and discussed under the headings of Strategy for Discovery, Tactics for Discovery, Personal Traits and Attitudes for Discoverers, Caveats, A Few Views and Comments on Science, The Inside Story of One Discovery, and Closing Remarks. These headings serve as an organizational framework, but the reader will quickly recognize that the boundaries of the categories are arbitrary and often breached. Some guidelines could just as well be placed under a different heading. Such ambiguity in classification is unavoidable but should not be detrimental. Most of the guidelines are self-standing; i.e., they can be read, or referred to, without one's also reading other parts of the book.

To make the book easy to comprehend, a simple pattern is adhered to. For each guideline, there is a heading that is brief and to some extent self-explanatory. The heading is followed by one or a few paragraphs of explanation of the point. Next, where appropriate, examples are given to illustrate the point. This arrangement is generally consistent throughout the book and gives the reader the option of skimming, delving selectively, or reading comprehensively.

It is obvious that subjective judgment on my part is involved throughout this book and particularly in the selection of the various guidelines for discussion. It is, with no apologies, a subjective book about a subjective subject. Some points are probably controversial. Some readers will be stimulated to think of favorite guidelines of their own that they would like to bring to the attention of others. If so, they will quickly come to recognize that, beyond the small, informal, oral discussion group, science provides few forums for consideration of such matters. There should be more.

A Little Background in Earth Science

FOR those who are not well versed in earth science, this section presents a brief historical framework as a setting for the examples in the text. As a history, this section is, of course, highly oversimplified. Earth science is too large and too broad a subject to be described comprehensively here or almost anywhere for that matter.

To make the subject manageable and directly relevant to what follows, this section focuses on efforts and events that led, or contributed, to an understanding of geology *in a global sense*. Taking the global view allows us to bypass much specialized material and much information of primarily local or regional significance and to concentrate on the great developments in global tectonics during the 1960s when earth science experienced its most fertile period ever for major discovery. I begin at the beginning however, and outline the development of collective geological thought. The reasoning of individuals is left largely to the examples cited in later sections.

Geology, like its companion subject geography, must have begun with the advent of curiosity in humans. "What is there?" is the basic question of geography. "What is it made of?" and

"How did it get that way?" are the basic questions of geology. To answer those childlike but fundamental queries has always been the prime goal of basic earth science. The answers were initially slow in coming.

The earth was four and a half billion years old and humans in some form had lived on earth for a few million of those years before any single human, or any organism, learned what the entire surface of the earth looks like! That single fact is a dramatic example of the spectacular advances in understanding that characterize the era in which we live. The last few hundred years have brought a remarkable increase in knowledge of the earth. To comprehend the entire earth was not an available opportunity during most of human existence.

But once geographical exploration of the earth in a global sense began, it was over in an instant of geological time. Just a few hundred years ago, it was possible, with only modest effort, to discover a new continent, a new sea, a new island arc, or a new river system. What a marvelous time for the aspiring discoverer! There was a great frontier. It was easy to recognize. It was not overly difficult to conquer.

Now that opportunity is gone, completely gone. There are no more seas or continents to discover. All parts of the earth's surface are known. If we need additional information on some locality, a satellite flying overhead will make daily pictures of it. So far as the configuration of the surface of the earth is concerned, we pretty well know "What is there." There are other challenges in the science of geography, of course, but learning the shape of the surface for the first time is no longer one of them.

We also know a great deal about what the surficial rocks are made of. For several hundred years, geologists have studied the land area of the earth, walking over most of it in the process. Although much detailed work remains, in a broad sense we already have rather comprehensive information on rocks of the surface. We have maps that tell us what kinds and what ages of rocks are found almost everywhere on land. The collection and compilation of that information is a magnificent accomplishment. It is an achievement that required innumerable hours of field observation by countless scientists, all marvelously driven, in spite of their different cultures, languages, and backgrounds, toward a common goal: the understanding of the earth. Comprehensive information on the surficial rocks of the continents was available, more or less, well before the early 1940s, the time of World War II. That great war marked a turning point in the history of humanity and also in the history of geology. I shall come to that in a moment. First, let us see what the first round of geological observation of the earth revealed and what ideas it provoked.

Some very basic facts about the earth were evident from reconnaissance-scale global geological information. For one thing, it was clear that exposed rocks vary in character substantially from place to place. The earth is round and smooth in global perspective, but the rocks of the surface are diverse and lacking in any obvious spherical symmetry. Nevertheless, the variations are neither random nor incomprehensible; they form organized, recognizable patterns. And, blessedly, some of the patterns are of large scale, often thousands of kilometers in linear dimension.

Furthermore, the rocks are commonly, though not always, deformed. Many have been changed from their original configuration through folding and faulting of, typically, flat-lying layers of sediments or igneous rocks. Sometimes deformation has occurred to the same rocks more than once, but usually not more than a few times. The fact of deformation and the great scale of some of the deformed features are critical clues. They tell us that a process of large, perhaps global, scale has deformed the earth, and likely is still deforming it.

But what is that process? That question, essentially "How did it get that way?" did not escape the attention of early geologists. They sought the mechanism of deformation. Their evidence came from dry land geology; that was all that was known. Many ideas and variations of ideas developed. Most were not sufficiently visionary to endure for long. However, one particular style became more popular than others. Scientists were caught up in what became the prevailing thinking of the time, a mode we now call "fixist," and it was in error.

Perhaps it was the subconscious psychological influence of personal experience with the solid and enduring character and the huge masses and volumes of rocks coupled with the recognition of the great age of the earth, one of geology's greatest achievements, that led many early earth scientists to become fixists. Fixists thought that rocks remained more or less near the place where they were formed throughout their history (and hence were "fixed"). Fixists accepted the notion that rock deformation was evidence of vertical or horizontal movements of a few kilometers but rejected the possibility of lateral movement large enough to be significant on a global scale. The reason for rejection was simply that it could not be demonstrated that the rocks had moved through long distances. Hence the rocks, they thought, must have remained fixed. In retrospect, it is easy to see fallacious logic in that conclusion. It could not be demonstrated that they had moved, but it could not be demonstrated that they had not moved either! Both possibilities should have been kept open. Nevertheless, most chose the simpler option (see Chapter 5 on the dangers of Occam's razor) and fixism prevailed.

In order to explain the evolution of rocks to their present state, considerable attention was directed toward the contraction theory during the fixist period. According to this theory, the earth was molten during an early stage of its history. As it cooled, a crust formed at the surface, and the earth's volume contracted. As the surface area shrank, the solid rocks of the crust were deformed. Prominent mountain belts, for example, were a consequence of compressional deformation of specific zones and hence a sign of cooling of the whole. The contraction theory was widely recognized for many decades. Lord Kelvin's erroneous calculations on the age of the earth, which misled the science for decades, were based on the cooling of the earth as envisioned in the contraction theory.

Not all early earth scientists were fixists, however. A few held other views. Another school, now called the mobilists, gradually developed. Generally in the minority before the 1960s, the mobilists held that rocks could travel through large distances. Perhaps the original, or at least an early, mobilist was the unknown who saw the first realistic maps of the Atlantic coasts of Africa and South America, noted the jigsawlike fit, and suspected that they might once have been together. That simple but great idea, which must have been had by many on seeing those maps, was hardly an instant success in the earth science community. Partly that was because of fixation on fixism. Partly it was a consequence of a prevailing attitude that emphasized observation to the exclusion of weakly supported theory or hypothesis. Theories of global tectonics were not spelled out well, or dwelled upon, in the early days. It must have been that many geologists ignored theories, dismissed them as arm waving, or considered them as conversation items and little else. One man took it upon himself to change that, and so he did, but not immediately, and not until he was assisted following his death by a great new set of observations.

In the early twentieth century, the premier mobilist entered the scene. His name was Alfred Wegener and he was a German meteorologist and astronomer, not a geologist. Wegener was taken by the idea that the continents had drifted over long distances. Although others had had related thoughts earlier, they had not presented them persuasively or pursued them thoroughly. Wegener went at the task with a vengeance. He explored every facet of the subject that he could. He lectured frequently and published papers and books. He probed the subject in depth and breadth. In the process, he uncovered, and drew attention to, a great variety of evidence, much of which remains valid today as support for continental drift. Wegener knew what to do. He knew how to get attention for his ideas and he did. He is more than deserving of his sometime title "Father of Continental Drift."

Wegener did not, however, enjoy general or immediate acceptance of his concept. And it is an important lesson in the way that science works to recognize that he did not and why he did not. There were some early supporters to be sure, but there were more detractors. So-called authoritative geological opinion went against him. This response may have been the result of the psychological attraction of fixism, or general inertia in scientific thought, or the appeal and weight of leaders of the opposition, but it was also because parts of Wegener's story were incorrect.

In particular Wegener erred when he claimed that the continents drifted through rocks of the ocean floor, somewhat like rafts through water. We now know that the continents, which are weak, do indeed move, but the sea floor, which is strong, does not part to make way for them. Wegener's contemporaries raised this valid objection to his theory. Nor did Wegener propose a satisfactory mechanism to cause the continents to drift as he claimed they had. When these parts of his story were attacked and demonstrated to be lacking, his basic concept of continental drift faltered and was held in abeyance until new evidence arose to provide strong support for the essence of his theory reset in modified form. Wegener died in the meantime, but he had made his ideas so widely known that they could not be brushed aside forever, as the imaginative ideas of others have so often been. Wegener's ideas appeared in 1912 and were elaborated and debated heavily over the next decade or more.

There followed a period during which, as best as I can discern, only a handful of visionary leaders of the science continually pondered the problems of global tectonics. But the average geologist did not, judged from the literature of, say, the 1920s and 1930s. In any case, no great progress in global tectonics was made during this period. To a very limited few, however, it became apparent that (1) in order to study global phenomena, global data were necessary and that (2) there were huge gaps in the global data. Land geology had become reasonably well known, but almost nothing was known of the ocean basins that span two thirds of the earth's surface.

But recognizing the deficiency was one thing. Doing something about this huge task was another. Strangely, World War II was the catalyst that stimulated the additional data gathering that geology needed.

World War II, among other things, produced an unprecedented shake-up of society. Humans, mostly young men, were
transported, with little choice on their part, from normal surroundings to the far corners of the earth. They had to carry out
tasks that they had not chosen, that required the learning of
new skills, and that provided new kinds of experiences. They
learned how to survive and travel and work under conditions
that, in the absence of the wartime effort, they might never have
encountered. Millions were so reoriented and broadened. Of those
millions, a few were already committed to science before their
wartime service. A small number of others would return from the
war to begin careers in science. Horrible as that war was, it
nevertheless produced as a side effect a core of young scientists
with uncommonly broad, diverse, and sometimes global, experience outside the realm of formal science.

Included in this group were some who were fascinated by the
adventure, the challenge, and the opportunity of exploring the
great earth science frontier of the post–World War II era, the
ocean basins. They brought a new thrust to earth science, a new
raison d'être. They expanded the scope of existing oceanographic
institutions, or formed new ones, and set about the task of
exploring the sea floor in every feasible way. It was a huge under-
taking, but in the surprisingly short time of less than two decades, it produced results that exceeded the grandest dreams of
the participants. Particularly prominent in this effort were a
group at Cambridge University led by Sir Edward Bullard, scientists from the established Scripps Institute of Oceanography and
Woods Hole Oceanographic Institution, and an upstart group at
Columbia University, led by Maurice Ewing, that would evolve
into the Lamont-Doherty Geological Observatory. Other groups
and individuals also contributed. All were aided by the dawn of
a new era of federal funding of science and by wartime development of military devices that could be converted into scientific instruments. Data in great quantity and great variety began
to accumulate. There were echo soundings of the sea floor, seismic soundings of buried rocks, gravity and magnetic field
measurements, dredgings and cores of the ocean bottom, and
photographs of the sea floor. Specialists filling the spectrum
from theoretical geophysicist to micropaleontologist participated. Gradually a new view of the ocean basins emerged. It

was critical to the development of understanding of global tectonics.

But, not all the important action of the post–World War II era was at sea. Geologists expanded their study of rocks of the continents. One group of geophysicists found an especially provocative and productive track. They studied paleomagnetism, i.e., the magnetic field locked into rocks at the time they were formed and with an orientation like the earth's field at that time. They found that measurements on many continents were consistent with the mobilists' idea of drifting continents and not with the fixists' view. These studies of the 1950s and early 1960s gave new impetus to the story of continental drift but for a time they drew the attention only of the avant-garde. Runcorn, Irving, and Bullard were among the key scientists in this subject.

The paleomagnetic studies on land took another direction as well. It concerned variations in the earth's magnetic field with time. Eventually studies of layered volcanic rocks, notably one by Cox, Doell, and Dalyrymple, revealed to everyone's surprise that the earth's field has frequently reversed polarity in the past. And a record of reversals through time was worked out. The intervals between reversals are irregular but are typically measured in hundreds of thousands of years. These magnetic studies would suddenly fall into place with the work at sea in a fashion beyond anyone's wildest dreams. Together they became the key to the solution of the great question "How did it get that way?" But work had to progress at sea, as well as on land, before the connection could be made.

During the post–World War II era, change in study of the ocean basins was rapid in almost every respect—style, facilities, observations, and understanding. At first, some incorrect ideas based on extrapolation of land geology into the ocean basins had to be overturned and discarded. For example, it had to be demonstrated that rocks of the ocean crust are unlike those of the continental crust, and hence, that land bridges had not appeared and disappeared and continental masses had not sunk beneath the sea. It had to be shown that the Pacific basin was not the birthplace of the moon. Then it was discovered by Ewing and Heezen that a continuous mountain range and rift encircled the globe like stitches on a baseball. It was mostly beneath the sea; it was twice the earth's circumference in length! Such a huge feature demanded an explanation through a mechanism of global scale.

In the early 1960s, Harry Hess, a Princeton professor with a distinctly maverick style, proposed that new sea floor was created at this great rift and spread to the sides as magma welled into the rift from below and that the continents were drifting apart as the sea floor grew. Although others had had similar thoughts earlier, Hess's idea went beyond them and was both masterful and timely. It was timely because the work at sea was producing some dramatic evidence that would support Hess's idea.

The evidence came from the study of magnetic anomalies, the differences between the observed field and the theoretical field. In some places the field was stronger than theory predicted, in others weaker. The spatial pattern of the anomalies was the key. Maps revealed a striped pattern of high and low magnetic anomalies. The stripes are normally parallel to a ridge (or rift, or spreading center), and typically each stripe is tens of kilometers in width. The observed geometric pattern of the stripes is uniform and highly organized. The incredibly simple pattern seemed out of place in a world in which geologists had come to anticipate complexity and irregularity in rocks that often seem just short of chaos.

An explanation for the simple magnetic pattern came quickly. It was proposed by Vine and Matthews in England and Morley in Canada. It showed that the magnetic data strongly supported the ideas of sea floor spreading and continental drift. The hypothesis was also a prime example of beauty in simplicity. As the sea floor parted, it postulated, molten rocks welled up to fill the gap and then froze, adding to the surface area and locking in the magnetic polarity at the time of magma emplacement, freezing, and cooling through the Curie temperature. The process continued as spreading continued, with each segment of sea floor moving out to make room for the new. But the magnetic field reversed from time to time. Thus rocks of the sea floor traveling away from the spreading center carried, in the striped pattern, a record of the reversing field. The faster the spreading, the more surface area created between reversals. Hence, the broader the stripes. The sea floor, it turned out, is a stupendous magnetic tape recorder. Any particular stripe can be identified with a particular episode of magnetic polarity by counting stripes from a modern spreading center outward. Hence the age of the sea floor at that stripe can be determined from its place in the magnetic field history. The sea-floor-spreading hypothesis was confirmed and the sea floor anywhere could be dated simply by determining which stripe it carried. The age of the sea floor, it turned out, increases with distance from a spreading center.

There is, however, no very old sea floor. The greatest age of sea floor anywhere is about two hundred million years, less than the last 5 percent of earth history. The continents, on the other hand, have rocks as old as four billion years, twenty times the age of the oldest rocks of the oceans. The ocean basins are young, the continents much older. There had to be something that rejuvenates ocean rocks, while preserving at the surface at least some of the rocks of the continents. That something was revealed as the investigations proceeded further.

The spreading centers are not simple linear features. They have linear segments, but the segments are commonly offset, so that there is a rectilinear pattern to the spreading centers, or rifts, and the intervening ridges, or faults. This rectilinear pattern was confounding, until Tuzo Wilson proposed the transform fault hypothesis. The ridges that link the spreading centers are associated with faults that adjust the spreading at one segment of the rift to that of a nearby but offset segment. The hypothesis neatly explains the observed effects in a way that is compatible with sea floor spreading and magma upwelling. Lynn Sykes quickly confirmed Wilson's important hypothesis through the use of earthquake data.

Once it was recognized that the sea floor is young, that it spreads, and that new surface material is created at the rifts, a major new problem arose. Does the earth expand to accommodate the new surface area? Or is surface material being removed in some manner elsewhere? In answer, some suggested that surface material sinks into the interior beneath the continents, or beneath the trenches of island arcs, or in poorly specified fashion at widely distributed locations elsewhere. Bryan Isacks and I, using seismic data from the Tonga-Fiji region, were able to show that the island arc hypothesis was the correct one and that surface material disappears at island arcs as plates of the earth's strong outer layer, or lithosphere, descend into the interior in a process now called subduction (see Chapter 7).

With processes for creation and destruction of crustal material in hand, a critical step remained. It was necessary to show that the spatial pattern of spreading, transform faulting, and subduction was self-consistent globally and compatible with known features of the earth. Jason Morgan, a young Princeton professor, made this important step. He postulated a mosaiclike pattern of a half dozen lithospheric plates that cover the entire earth's surface and, on the assumption that they are rigid, showed that their relative motions are consistent with other kinds of observations. The global scheme was revealed. Confirmation and extension of the theory followed. Xavier LePichon plotted quantitative global plate motions. Isacks, Sykes, and I fitted all relevant earthquake data to the model, refining it in the process. Oxburgh and Turcotte provided a theory of compatible convective flow in the interior. Dewey and Bird related dry land geology, mostly mountain building and associated phenomena, to plate tectonics. A theory that in its earliest stages had emphasized marine areas became globally comprehensive. Plate tectonics was established and going strong by 1970, less than a quarter of a century after World War II spawned a new crop of earth scientists with a different outlook on observing the earth.

In 1962, Kuhn published his now well-known, innovative ideas about the conduct and history of science. Most of the time, he said, scientists work at "puzzle solving," trying to fit observations into the existing framework of science in that era. Kuhn called that framework a paradigm. Occasionally, he said, an existing paradigm becomes inadequate. Then science experiences a major upheaval as a new paradigm is formed. Afterward, the science reverts again to puzzle solving, but now under the rules of the new paradigm. Although Kuhn's ideas were based largely on the history of physics, his characterization fits what has happened to earth science extremely well. Plate tectonics, with its mobilist theme, was clearly a major new paradigm. It was preceded by a puzzle-solving era in which the paradigm of fixism prevailed.

Furthermore, at present it seems clear that earth science has reverted once again to the puzzle-solving stage, this time under the plate tectonics paradigm. Advances are made often in modern geology, but just now there is neither a sense nor the substance of a revolution comparable to that of plate tectonics.

Many scientists are content to operate in the puzzle-solving mode. In some ways that seems the natural pace of science— long intervals of puzzle solving interspersed with brief intervals of upheaval and paradigm discovery. But is there really a fixed natural pace for science? Or can the tempo be sped up and the arrival of the next new paradigm hastened? I think, as some others do, that the tempo of science can be speeded by modifying the style of science. That conviction is the basis for this book, which aims to instill in young scientists a taste for the paradigm rather than the puzzle. That taste is the counterpart in the scientific process to what is sometimes called, in other circles and in less civilized fashion, the instinct for the jugular.

How can we accelerate the pace to the next paradigm? The answer to that question seems obvious, given the principles on which this book is based. If we can discover by following the example of past discoverers, perhaps we can find a new paradigm by following the pattern of previous paradigm discovery.

The preceding encapsulated history of the finding of the paradigm of plate tectonics suggests how to do it or at least one way to do it. The formula is remarkably simple. Identify an important frontier. Explore that frontier. Observe the unknown thoroughly.

Discovery and new ideas will almost certainly result. We need only to identify the next major frontier, the counterpart of the ocean basins of the 1950s, and explore it. A major new advance will almost certainly follow. What is that frontier? Each leader of science must decide that independently. However, on surveying the subject, one answer seems obvious to me. The next frontier is the buried continental crust. Humans have explored the surface of the land and the surface and depths of the sea. Now detailed exploration of the interior is in order and the nearby relatively shallow but buried continental crust is obviously next in line.

Like the ocean basins of the 1950s, the buried continental crust, some 40 km thick, is both huge and poorly known. Only the sedimentary basins, the province of petroleum, have been intensively investigated. Yet knowledge of the entire crust must be important to the understanding of global, certainly continental, geology. Surface geology of the land is reasonably well known, but beneath it lies the largely unknown third dimension of continental geology! What could be more important?

As in the case of the ocean basins after World War II, there are devices and techniques readily available for exploring the new frontier. We need only to mount the effort to apply them. And there are already many characteristic forerunners of a new paradigm in the form of observations of the buried crust that do not fall into place under the existing paradigm. The signs are all there and all positive. For humans to take the next major step in understanding the solid earth, it seems that all that remains is to do the job of exploring the deep crust comprehensively and to be alert for new perspectives and new unifying scientific concepts as that task of exploration progresses.

The Consortium for Continental Reflection Profiling (CO-CORP), with which I am involved, is an example of a project oriented to take advantage of this opportunity through deep seismic reflection profiling of the entire crust. Similar activities are being conducted by others throughout the world. The principal technique is an expanded version of the seismic method developed by the petroleum industry for exploring the sedimentary basins, although some also explore the crust using other techniques. The results so far are highly encouraging. There are already observations of many large new and surprising features, unexpected spatial consistencies in features of large scale, and similarities of deep features in widespread geographic locations. There is clearly a frontier full of major earth features and phenomena waiting to be revealed. There is a host of inconsistencies with existing paradigms. The subject may already be approaching the stage when the counterpart of Hess's proposal of sea floor spreading can be visualized by someone, somewhere.

Understanding of the continental crust, in contrast to some other topics in science, will inevitably have important practical ramification for society as a whole. Whereas exploration of the earth's deeper interior, for example, is a fine intellectual target and one worthy of scientists' attention, understanding of the core can hardly be expected to have the same impact on society as will understanding of the crust, the home and the source of livelihood for humans. Furthermore, as in cosmology, studies of the remote deep interior of the earth must rely heavily on imaginative theory because observations of these inaccessible regions are difficult to make and inherently limited. The buried crust cannot be observed as thoroughly as the surface, of course, but it is amenable to study with techniques of much higher resolution than can be applied to the deeper regions. It is, furthermore, the link between the surface that supports life and the internal regions and processes below.

But the continental crust is by no means the only frontier of earth science. Opportunities for discovery of new paradigms must exist elsewhere in earth science and in other sciences. The impact of extraterrestrial bodies to account for such features as the iridium anomaly at the Cretaceous-Tertiary boundary is an example of a possible new paradigm. Whether that paradigm will become established is uncertain at this writing.

The preceding brief history of global earth science gives a woefully incomplete record of the subject. Many important contributions and contributors are omitted. But it should provide some background on the general flow of the subject for those uninitiated in earth science and, hence, provide a setting for some of the examples in the rest of the book.

One cannot consider the history of a science without asking what that history suggests for the future. I have already made comments on a few imminent developments. Over the next few decades, or perhaps centuries, the exciting period of human exploration of the earth will continue. In the longer term, say some hundreds of years, I see a lessening of opportunity for major discovery about the earth. Many of my colleagues would disagree with this view. However, I think the parallel with geography is apt. Once most of what can be observed is observed, and the data organized and reorganized a few times, the important observations will be accounted for and the important discoveries achieved. Only matters of lesser significance will then remain to be discovered, just as now there are no longer opportunities to discover continents or seas in geography. Of course, the need for practitioners of earth science will continue and society will demand and find new ways to make use of the earth.

But geology in a few centuries will have passed through its major discovery period and at that time would-be discoverers should go elsewhere. At present, however, it is clear that there are many major discoveries remaining to be made in geology (see Chapter 3), for the simple reason that there are many things remaining to be observed. The modern student of earth science can be assured of an exciting time if he or she can position himself or herself to be associated with those discoveries. How to do that is what the rest of the book is about.

For those who would like to read a more nearly complete history of the discovery of plate tectonics, a wide variety of choices is available. Some of those histories were written by participating scientists, some by scientists who were on the periphery of the action, some by science historians and science writers. No history portrays the past quite like those who experienced it now remember it, for each of us saw it in a different way and from his or her own perspective. However, some of the available histories give a reasonable and thorough account of how the subject of plate tectonics developed. I like the histories by Marvin, Coulomb, and Allegre among others. At least one such history, though, which shall be nameless here, is often a figment of the author's imagination and yet it purports to be a factual account. That one infuriates me. A supposed factual history is not the place to display a talent for fiction.

I especially like Menard's *Ocean of Truth*. Menard carries the story only through the discovery of sea floor spreading. However, with the experience of a participant he is able to give a realistic portrayal of how various events occurred and were viewed at that time, at least from the perspective of the laboratory at which he worked. For those who seek insight into the thought processes of scientists during this era of discovery, Menard's book may be the best. Recently some accounts of personal experience of scientists active in the discovery of plate tectonics have begun to appear. They are revealing of special topics but generally less comprehensive than Menard's text. Also recently two studies of continental drift and the plate tectonics revolution have appeared, one by LeGrand, a historian and philosopher of science, and the other by Stewart, a sociologist of science. I find both well done and interesting, but neither focused on the matter of how active scientists can do better as a consequence of the lessons of history.

All history is to some degree a story by the historian, and in that sense not a complete or fully accurate record of the past. Typically historians see the history of science in a light different from those who participated in that history. So too do scientists come to see history in a different light after participating in, and reading accounts of, a particular segment of history. There is no way to avoid the incomplete nature of history. We cannot ever expect to reproduce the past fully. But we can hope to focus our histories on certain matters that will be helpful to us in the future. The next chapter begins a discussion of guidelines for discovery in science based on lessons of the past found partly in written history but mostly in personal experience.

The guidelines are discussed one by one and in a style designed to convey the spirit of the guideline, as well as the content. How and when the guidelines shall be used and blended together is, naturally, an exercise for the individual in the course of a career.

HISTORY OF SCIENCE

AN EARLY EPISODE IN THE RIFT VALLEY OF AFRICA

2

3

T W O

Strategy for Discovery

THE perceptive reader will note that, although a later part of this book warns of the danger of losing useful information in classification schemes, such a scheme is used to organize the book! The dilemma is unavoidable. Some of the difficulties of classification are illustrated in this chapter, for many of the guidelines appearing in this chapter entitled Strategy for Discovery do not fit tidily under such a heading.

In spite of the difficulties with imperfect classification, a chapter on strategy seems appropriate if only to emphasize the importance of long-term strategical considerations in science and, in particular, the critical nature of their role in the mind of a discoverer. Although all the guidelines of this chapter have common ground, they are something of a mixed bag. Some are directed toward long-term personal styles and some toward long-term procedures or policies in scientific research. Some concern points that are already well known to most readers; others may not be so obvious to the beginner. Some will be accepted by most; others will be controversial, particularly with senior scientists who follow a different style. Some guidelines partially repeat points of other guidelines, but in such cases, an independent related point is made, so that the difference in emphasis and content justifies the limited overlap.

Strategy per se receives only limited attention in science. The term is more often, and perhaps better, applied in the military where the basic conflict is normally clear and the foe is well defined. In science, the unknown is the foe and it is not so well defined. Nevertheless, long-term considerations are appropriate in science and it is in that sense that the term *strategy* is used here to organize a group of guidelines.

Don't Follow the Crowd

THIS first guideline is an obvious and an all-encompassing one. In a way it is a summary of the entire book. Crowd following is comfortable, but it is not the way to exceptional achievement in science or anything else. A discoverer must think and act independently in order to reach a part of the unknown before others. Very talented people abound in science. Competition is keen. Unless you are a truly exceptional person, you will find it impossible to surpass all other scientists and reach a position of leadership while traveling in the mainstream. To attempt to do so will almost ensure that you will watch others make the major discoveries, if indeed there are any remaining to be made in the mainstream.

Fortunately, there is another way. In fact, there are many other ways. Science is not like a marathon with one starting place, one finish, and one route between. There are many places to start and innumerable routes to follow in science.

Instead of joining the crowd in sheeplike fashion, proceed differently. Learn first what the crowd is doing in the branch of science of interest. That part is easy. Science is organized to provide such information through scientific meetings, journals, books, etc. Use the system to find out what is going on. The next step is critical. Spend a substantial effort visualizing what that branch of science *might* be doing. This is a difficult step requiring vision and contemplation, but once achieved, it will then, of course, be evident what the crowd is *not* doing. A promising but unexplored direction may emerge. Once you see it, move boldly in that direction. If all goes well, the crowd will soon be following you, but likely not until after you have made the big discovery of the new direction.

This advice sounds so simple and straightforward as to be trite. Yet many scientists attend scientific meetings to learn, and be stimulated by, the news of latest developments in the field without giving any serious or prolonged thought to what is being overlooked by the crowd as it rushes pell-mell to solve the popular problems of the day. To seek and recognize those omissions is the trick that provides the edge.

To perceive what is not going on requires a somewhat detached point of view. It is not the view of the established mainstream worker. It is the view of the outsider who asks "What are the people in this branch of science doing *collectively?*" "What are the other things that might be done in this branch of science?" The intent of the exercise is not to be critical of the mainstream; normally the mainstream effort is more than adequately justified and does not deserve severe criticism. The intent is instead to seek out the promising new direction that languishes, a direction to pursue while the crowd focuses its attention elsewhere and follows a different course.

The capacity and the knack for revealing new scientific directions are well worthy of cultivation, not only because they open new access to discovery by the scientist but also because they generate an air of unpredictability and leadership for the individual that is advantageous in competition with fellow scientists.

Examples of major success by those who chose not to follow the crowd are so numerous and well known in all fields of science that they need little citation here. One example, already noted, stands out in earth science. Alfred Wegener, the great German meteorologist who in 1912 proposed the first comprehensive hypothesis on the drifting of continents, surely departed, and recognized that he was departing, radically from the mainstream of earth science of that era. Whether Wegener was stimulated more by the recognition that the mainstream left promising directions untouched or by his innate intuitive sense of how the earth might work is not the issue. Likely both factors were involved. But it is fully clear that he was decidedly not a crowd follower.

What triggered the development of plate tectonics in the 1960s was unquestionably the exploration of the ocean basins that followed World War II. Here the motivation is more clear. Leaders of the ocean exploration recognized that the mainstream of earth science at that time was directed toward study of the continents and that the great story of global geology could not be revealed without the addition of comprehensive information on the ocean floors. One of those leaders was Maurice Ewing, founder of the Lamont-Doherty Geological Observatory of Columbia University. He was decidedly not a crowd follower. Neither were Richard Field and Walter Bucher, professors of geology at Princeton and Columbia, respectively, who encouraged Ewing to study the sea floor. Both of these senior geologists were frustrated by attempts to understand global tectonics based solely on data from the continents, and they sensed that the sea floor was the great frontier, in effect, the missing link of global geology. Ewing combined an intense desire to excel in science with a knack for seeing the basic flow of science through the frills and sophistication that misdirect others. He recognized the wisdom and importance of the advice he was offered. He foresaw the coming of a major revolution in geology and he moved decisively to take advantage of the opportunity to be a part of it by developing means for observing the sea floor. Ewing's bold move to explore the world's ocean basins was paralleled by similar efforts led by Roger Revelle of the Scripps Institute of Oceanography and Sir Edward Bullard of Cambridge University among others. The route to the unknown through the ocean floors was wide open for exploitation. The crowd was elsewhere looking at the dry land. Discovery piled upon discovery at sea to reach a climax with the coming of the concept of plate tectonics, unquestionably a major new paradigm for earth science and perhaps the greatest advance ever in earth science.

Does avoidance of the crowd ensure major discovery in science? Of course not. It merely improves one's chances. The path of science is strewn with failures of what once seemed great ideas and promising new directions. Fate and fortune will ever play a role in scientific discovery. But so will the wisdom and judgment of scientific leaders. Science is built upon past failures, as well as upon successes, and a select few of those with the boldness and daring to depart from convention will always lead the way.

Rebel, but Wisely

THE general thrust of this book is to encourage certain individuals to break free of the chains of convention, in effect to rebel against the status quo and the ordinary. It is not, however, an exhortation to rebel indiscriminately or to rebel simply for the sake of rebellion. Those seeking major discovery do not serve their purpose by adopting unsound positions no matter how unconventional or superficially appealing the position may be. Wisdom in the choice of an area in which to rebel is essential. And so is timing.

Some people seem born to innovate, others not. But likely only a small fraction of the potential innovators become accomplished innovators. An innovator can often be identified readily as such. The mark of the innovator is abhorrence of the overly familiar. Innovators are uneasy with the status quo. If you have that quality, you're lucky. Capitalize on it. It's a precious gift. But don't squander it on trivia. Don't just get an outlandish haircut or an unusual T-shirt or a strange car and then feel satisfied that you've shown that you're different. And don't jump to vociferous support of every poorly thought out, radical cause just to demonstrate that you are willing to take on the establishment. The world needs more than that from you if you are bright and gifted with the capacity to innovate.

Instead (or in addition, if you must have a 1936 Packard!) seek bigger game. Nurture that innovative spirit, and don't lose confidence in it or yourself. Act decisively and forcefully, but wisely. Set major discovery as your goal and never lose sight of it. Behave like a running back in football who idles along behind the line until he sees an opening and then darts through it with a burst of speed and momentum. Or like the investor who harbors funds while studying the market thoroughly until, upon identifying an early opportunity, boldly moves into it before the crowd. Or like the oil man who carefully evaluates every aspect of a prospect before boldly taking the risky step of expensive drilling. But have the courage to make the daring move in timely fashion when the opportunity appears.

In science, one can often idle for a time by doing routine science while concurrently searching for a major opportunity. However, once the opportunity for major discovery is evident, the scientist must move boldly and quickly to take advantage of it. Otherwise, like the running back, the scientist will be caught from behind and trampled to obscurity by the onrushing crowd of other scientists who have followed the lead toward the prize. There is always such a crowd. It cannot be held back. But it can be led by those who are daring and decisive.

When the first indications of plate tectonics and its overwhelming importance to earth science began to appear in the form of the concept of sea floor spreading, a few scientists recognized the opportunity for further advance at the early stage and moved boldly to capitalize on it. To do so they needed, in addition to the recognition of the opportunity, a means to capitalize, i.e., an idea for advancing the concept beyond its most preliminary stages.

Tuzo Wilson, a Canadian geophysicist with a long-standing interest in problems of large-scale tectonics, hit upon such an idea when he found the concept now known as the transform fault. It was a clever idea that explained certain geological observations in a manner completely contrary to the conventional explanation. It fit nicely and complemented the concept of the spreading sea floor as proposed earlier by Harry Hess. Wilson recognized the potential and moved boldly and decisively to make the concept known. He prepared crude cardboard models, sometimes in view of the audience, and, it seemed, lectured so often and in so many places that every earth scientist had an opportunity to learn of the concept. In so doing, he helped advance the science in an important way and provided an outstanding example of bold and timely action to capitalize on an unconventional idea.

Strive to Enhance Serendipity

SERENDIPITY, the gift of finding agreeable things not sought for, seems something that is bestowed by fate and hence beyond the control of humans. But one might say the same for a quick mind, or a muscular body, or a graceful carriage. Yet each of these, though a gift, can be enhanced by appropriate action—study, exercise, and athletics or dance. The gift of serendipity can also be enhanced. Scientists can improve their chances for discovery by appropriate action and by decisions based on principles such as those suggested in this book.

As one example, consider one of the foremost, proven tricks for enhancing serendipity in earth science. It is to associate oneself with new kinds of observations of what appear to be prominent yet unexplored or poorly understood features of the earth. In other words, the trick is simply to explore a new frontier.

History shows that exploring a new frontier almost always provides major surprise. Examples are innumerable. Columbus discovered America simply by observing a previously unknown part of the earth. Hess discovered sea floor spreading once the sea floor had been adequately observed. Darwin's voyage on the *Beagle* provided him with an unparalleled set of observations that led to his ideas on evolution. The observations were unparalleled, that is, until a similar but later voyage by Wallace led him independently to observations and then conclusions like those of

Darwin. Both men became aware of similar observations; both men came to similar conclusions. Becoming associated with the appropriate observations was clearly the key to great discovery.

Comprehensive observations of the magnetization of layered volcanic rocks of different ages led Cox, Doell, and Dalrymple to the conclusion that the earth's magnetic field has changed its polarity at times in the past. Being first to know the observations was once again rewarded with spectacular discovery.

Each of these examples, and there are many others, tells us that we can control our fate. We can make discoveries happen. We need not wait for the birth of a genius. We need only to think of a major feature or characteristic of the earth that has not yet been well observed and then make or acquire those observations. With a little luck, an important discovery will follow. Making the decision to acquire such observations and then carrying out the observational process is straightforward. Almost anyone reasonably skilled in science and sufficiently determined and dedicated can do it. Then, once the key observations are in hand, and known, the great idea will be had by someone, likely, though not necessarily, the observer. Although credit is often awarded to the scientist who has the great idea, in fact it is the perceptive observer who initiates the process. The observer should take satisfaction in the success that follows and, in a perfect world, would receive a share of the credit, sometimes the lion's share.

To continue with the example of the previous section, note that Maurice Ewing consciously followed the course prescribed above when he set out to explore the ocean basins. He knew the basins were so large that they had to be important to an understanding of global geology. He did not know what secrets the ocean basins held or that they would be the source of a great new theory of the earth. Nor did he have such a theory to test. But he was conscious of, and driven by, the generalization that observations of previously unknown features or phenomena nearly always reveal something of major importance. And, of course, what followed proved that he was correct. Although he was not the originator of the concept of plate tectonics, it was surely the observations of the ocean basins that triggered it. Or put in another way, serendipity was enhanced by a wise plan of action, in this case, as in many others, the taking of observations.

As noted earlier, the strategy of the COCORP project for seismic reflection profiling of the buried portions of the continental crust is based on similar reasoning and, in fact, on the example set by Ewing. This project, in which I am heavily involved, is in its early stages at present, but it has already produced many surprising discoveries. It seems inevitable that major changes in understanding of the continents and their evolution will take place as a store of comprehensive observations of the deep continental crust evolves. In fact, the COCORP project, and similar efforts elsewhere, are in the process of providing a clear-cut test of whether a program consciously designed to provide major upheaval in a branch of science will indeed do so.

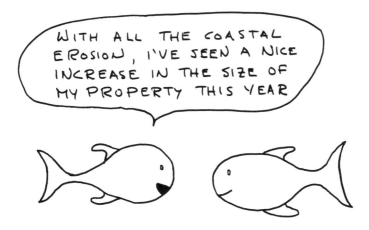

Avoid Science Eddies

SCIENTISTS often become so captivated by the intricacies and challenges of their day-to-day activities that they lose sight of their role, and those activities, in the larger context. In addition to playing the role of the specialist, it is important for scientists to develop a broad and detached perspective of science and to see their own work in that light.

With a little experience, it is easy to recognize that specialties in science can evolve into a state of increasing isolation. The practitioners lose touch with the flow and advance of science as a whole yet maintain a whirlpool of activity that consists largely of specialists talking to each other solely about that specialty. Like an eddy, such groups drift from the mainstream, maintaining an identity for a surprisingly long period. Eventually, however, and like an eddy, they commonly fade into obscurity.

To avoid being caught in such an eddy, it is important to develop a sufficiently broad perspective of science so that the eddy can be recognized. It is also important for the scientist working in a specialty to strive continually for interaction with specialists in different fields and with generalists. And it is vital to maintain a focus on the principal goals of the science, not just those of a particular specialty.

This guideline should not be interpreted to mean that a scientist should not specialize. To the contrary, specialization is almost essential in modern science. The guideline means instead that the scientist should evaluate a particular specialty in the larger context of science beyond the specialty and act according to that evaluation. In some cases the specialty can be reoriented so as to have impact on activity in other specialties; in some cases the individual should abandon the specialty and seek more fertile topics elsewhere, leaving the specialty to those unable to recognize its imminent decay.

Examples of specialties that have developed into science eddies are not hard to find.

One example from the past is the case of the Neptunists, those students and followers of Werner, the German geologist who attributed all rocks, including those now known to be igneous, to deposition from the primeval sea. As it became evident that some rocks were indeed volcanic in origin and Werner's ideas could not be correct, those who persisted in following and developing Werner's ideas made up an eddy that could then have been recognized and avoided, as it was by some. Most scientific eddies are not, however, so celebrated historically as Werner's.

I recall one trip to another country where I observed a laboratory bustling with activity as former students of a distinguished scientist, the since deceased director of the laboratory, strove to develop and expand the ideas of their former leader. Although once clever and ingenious, those ideas now seem hopelessly incorrect and out of date in modern science. Now they form the core of an eddy that seems destined for oblivion. The eddy is readily recognized by those more broadly based, but not by those who fail to cross the bounds of their early training.

Some readers will challenge the point of this section on the basis that occasionally in science a major new development will appear in a subject that otherwise, and to most, seemed devoid of consequence. Of course, that view is correct. Discoveries sometimes do come from unexpected places. But that fact is not sufficient justification for laboring on and on in a field that shows none of the characteristics of a subject ready to produce something important, characteristics such as, for example, an abundance of poorly understood observations of a feature of obvious importance. A certain amount of drudgery is often the key to success in science, but it is not a guarantee to success, and the message of this section is that scientists must continually reevaluate their positions to ensure that their efforts are in a field with promise.

Study the Earth *and* the Science of Geology

AT first glance, this guideline seems like double-talk. The science of geology is study of the earth, isn't it? Well, there is an area of overlap, of course, but the two topics are not identical. In some ways they are distinctly different.

The earth is a nice object to study. It is always there. It is well behaved. It faithfully and consistently responds to our efforts to obtain information about it. The earth is complicated and confounding, but it is not capricious.

The science of geology, like all sciences, is less reliable. Sometimes it describes the real earth, but then only in qualified terms. Mostly, geology is about an imaginary earth that exists only in the minds of scientists. The imaginary earth is something like the real earth and presumably grows more like it as the science progresses, but it is always at best an approximation and a fiction.

Furthermore, the science of geology has humans in it with the erratic and capricious behavior that they all share. Science is a human endeavor and a product of humans. The strengths and the frailties of humans are inextricably a part of any science, and those who study the science do well to recognize this aspect of the subject.

Thus a scientific paper, or a scientific conclusion, is not always, perhaps not often, carried out in the most objective, straightforward manner. To do so may have been the intent, and to have done so the conviction, of the author, but reality may differ. In spite of the noblest of intentions, and especially when a scientist is straining to pierce the frontier, human strengths and weaknesses become an important part of the science.

It is essential, therefore, that the scientist see and evaluate the works of other scientists (and if possible his or her own works as well) in light of the spirit of the times, the surroundings, the emotions, the personality, the character, and the personal history of the scientist. It is often useful to know about the childhood history, the educational history, the most influential professors, the fellow students, the recent achievements or setbacks, the recent marital history, the general level of personal integrity, and the extracurricular activities of a contributing scientist. Such things bear on the lives of all of us and many may be factors influencing indirectly and subconsciously the nature and quality of what appears in a scientific publication. It does no good to pretend otherwise.

To understand a science, then, one must try to know and understand scientists as a group and as individuals. It is an interesting task, for scientists are stimulating, talented, and lively people full of new ideas and diverse experiences. But those human factors play a role in the state and evolution of the science and it behooves every scientist to use that subjective information in the personal evaluation of the science.

I can recall an unusual example in which the normally admirable traits of kindness, generosity, and goodwill contrived to retard a branch of science. A senior scientist of proven accomplishment published a series of papers that at first seemed to provide beautiful confirmation and extension of a then-popular theory to which he subscribed. As time went on, however, it turned out that the observations on which the papers were based could not be duplicated by others and were likely false. The papers were therefore incorrect and misleading. The scientist was befuddled. He felt the data were reliable because they had been collected by carefully trained military personnel. He had no intent to mislead, and he had not knowingly falsified anything. Eventually it was revealed that the scientist, a friendly and lovable older man, was so endearing to the young military personnel, who were not indoctrinated in the objectivity of science, that they took great pains to make certain that the data they collected revealed what the scientist hoped would be revealed. They were, they felt, being helpful, not malicious. They acted naively and improperly but with good intent. He acted with good intent. But the differences and the inadequacies of humans combined to throw science off the track. Given a less likable scientist, and observers of different persuasion, this example of the effect of personal traits on a science would not have occurred. But it did, and the science had to be righted by those who took account of the foibles of humans.

The message of this section is by no means exclusive to study of the earth. The title of this section might equally well have been "Study life, *and* the science of biology," or "Study physical phenomena *and* the science of physics," or "Study celestial bodies *and* the science of astronomy." Wherever humans are involved in science, and that is everywhere in science, the essence of this section applies. Science is a structure built by humans with all the complications that phrase implies.

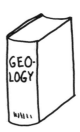

Seek the Nonquestions

BY nonquestions I mean questions that might be asked about some branch of science but that somehow are ignored or forgotten. Thus the solutions are not actively sought. By recogniz-ing such questions and pursuing them, a scientist may find an easy path to discovery. This guideline might be thought of, then, as a special case of "Don't follow the crowd," but listing it sep-arately places emphasis on a particular way of bypassing the crowd.

There is nothing new about the basic principle of this guide-line. High school science teachers so often draw attention to the need to "ask the right questions" that the expression has become a cliché. But those who develop a knack for seeking questions at the high school level may fail to recognize that the same tech-nique can be applied at much higher levels of science and for much greater stakes.

During the period of enlightenment that accompanied the development of the plate tectonics paradigm, many examples of earlier failures to ask the right questions became evident. In the mid-1960s, I became involved, with colleagues Bryan Isacks and Lynn Sykes, in an effort to relate all of the observational data of earthquake seismology to the evolving concept of plate tectonics. (The concept was in an early stage and not known by that name at the time. We referred to it by our own term "the new global tectonics.") It was obvious that the pattern of worldwide seis-micity had to be a key piece of evidence in any study of global tectonics. Stimulated by our interests, Muawia Barazangi and James Dorman produced global maps of epicenters with unprec-edented accuracy of location. Those valuable maps became the basis for many tectonics studies. Their accuracy and clarity made them especially useful. Nevertheless, well before this period of rapid advance, maps such as those found in Gutenberg and Richter's "Seismicity of the Earth" and a similar study by Rocard in France had clearly revealed the same basic global pattern of the seismic belts.

But seismologists of the earlier era (including the author!) had somehow bypassed some key questions that could have been answered by the global seismicity pattern and, hence, had over-looked an opportunity to make major advances in the under-standing of tectonics. For example, the observations showed that the belts of seismicity were essentially continuous and that a belt was nearly always terminated in truncation by another belt. The belts, in fact, had the appropriate pattern to outline what we have come to recognize as the boundaries of the plates. Furthermore, the pattern has certain other characteristics that make it distinctive. It is embarrassingly easy to recognize such features now, but before the mid-1960s we neglected to ask ourselves why the pattern had that particular configuration. Seismic belts never crossed other belts, for example. Intersections of belts, in other words, always involved three segments, not four or more. We could have, and should have, asked "why?" in the 1950s. But somehow the "why" was a nonquestion then, and we never focused our attention on that observation.

Likewise in the 1950s we knew that deep earthquakes occurred only in certain segments of the seismic belts, but we neglected to ask ourselves why that particular global pattern of deep seismicity appeared. It took the burst of enlightenment of the 1960s to lead us to that question. It may be too much to argue that we could have discovered plate tectonics in the 1950s on the basis of known global earthquake patterns, but it is not too much to affirm that the question of why those patterns had the appearance they did should have been asked.

As another example, consider the key discovery of the principle of the transform fault, a topic already mentioned in an earlier guideline. Before the 1960s students were taught about a particular class of fault with a vertical fault plane and purely horizontal motion. It was, and still is, called a strike-slip, or transcurrent fault. The type example of such faulting occurred during the 1906 San Francisco earthquake. From that event, we were able to observe the sense and magnitude of the maximum displacement (right-lateral and more than 20 feet) along a part of the great San Andreas Fault, which was already known as a major structural fracture. Little was said, however, about what happens near the ends of the region of faulting. The question was bypassed. It became a "nonquestion." Often a textbook illustration of such a strike-slip fault terminated without ever reaching the "end" of the fault. It was, conveniently, off the page! As Tuzo Wilson would show later, and as cited earlier, what happens at the ends is critical. New surface material appears from below there or disappears into the interior there. That is the basis for the transform fault hypothesis. To our chagrin, we hid that discovery behind a nonquestion for many years.

Stop reading here for a while and see if you can think of some nonquestions in your branch of science as it operates at present. A discovery may be waiting.

See Your Era in Long-Term Perspective

OVER the short term, progress in science often seems painfully slow. Weeks, months, even years sometimes go by without major progress on a particular project. A scientist whose only perspective is based on a single project may come to see science as a rather static activity and may be lulled into a state approaching hibernation. However, a longer term and broader perspective invariably reveal science as a much more dynamic and stimulating subject, with advances here, there, and elsewhere adding up to continual rapid progress.

Furthermore, viewing modern science in historical perspective often reveals trends leading to opportunities in the future. A researcher should know how his or her branch of science evolved to its present state. Patterns of changes from the past to the present often extrapolate into the future. He or she should speculate on what it will be like in that branch of science five, ten, twenty-five, or one hundred years from now. Recognizing change, and rate of change, is essential to predicting new direction in science. And positioning oneself for the next stage is an important part of discovery-oriented research.

Looking back over a few decades reveals an astonishing rate of change in science. Consider earth science as an example. When I was a graduate student, the earth was thought to be two billion years younger than the four-and-a-half-billion-year age we assign it today. The earth aged two billion years while I aged forty! No humans had been to the moon, or to the tops of the highest mountains, or to the great depths of the sea. Geologists have now been to all of those places. The Pacific was thought to be the scar left from the birth of the moon. Land bridges across oceans were said to come and go to provide transportation routes for land organisms. Now we know that the Pacific Basin is too young for lunar motherhood and that the continents drift about carrying passengers like ferry boats rather than like bridges.

Such recollections are not purely nostalgic memories. They are the basis for foresight and for hope and daring in plotting a scientific program for the future.

A few years ago, a prominent female vocalist with a big band of the 1930s and 1940s was interviewed by a TV talk-show host. The host opened with the most routine of questions and got a sparkling and provocative reply. "What was it like to be a part of the big-band era of popular music?" he asked. She answered, "Well, if I'd known it was going to be an era, I would have paid more attention to it!"

Like that vocalist, most of us fail to recognize the special qualities of the present era until after it is long past. Those who do, however, may capitalize on its peculiar properties and on the trends leading to the next era and so develop or sustain leadership in that new era.

The history of human exploration of the earth in a global sense provides the basis for an example of the value of the long-term perspective. Human exploration of the earth began with geographical exploration. Initially it must have been confined to the vicinity of the dwelling place. But eventually it spread from neighborhood to province to region to an entire continent. Then a particular group of humans radiated from Europe not only to encompass the entire earth but also to communicate widely the results of their travels. In the short time of a few hundred years, geographical exploration of the entire earth's surface was completed. Geological exploration of the surface lagged only a little behind and soon geological mapping on a reconnaissance basis was largely achieved for the land-covered areas of the world. By the end of World War II, as noted earlier, the ocean basins had become the prime frontier of geological exploration, and in a few decades, this task was well in hand on a reconnaissance basis. This broad historical perspective clearly indicates that, so far as earth alone is concerned, attention will now turn to the next major unknown, the interior. It seems obvious that the buried portions of the continents are the next step in this continuing, and seemingly relentless, progression in human exploration and understanding. A scientist with a broad perspective of the past can, like an experienced surfer, see advancing waves and, at the appropriate time, join that wave and ride it to success in discovery.

The long-term perspective on human exploration of the earth of the previous paragraph suggests a "law" of the Murphy's law type. This law of science states "Anything of significance that can be observed will be observed." The law seems applicable throughout the sciences. It seems independent of any particular philosophy of science. It carries special significance for those who see, as I do, the essence of science solely as organization of observations. And it makes clear that those who are able to discern patterns in the progress of observing will also be finding patterns in the progress of discovery. Discovery follows observation of the unknown, but it is not far behind. And by perceiving the progression of exploration, one can position oneself to make the next discovery.

Go with Intuition

MANY scientists, although some more than others, are gifted with a special feeling for how nature works. They somehow sense that one explanation for a phenomenon is correct, another incorrect, and they seem able to guess what an unprecedented experiment or a new observation will reveal and to be correct an uncanny percentage of the time. We say they are blessed with good intuition.

Intuition is difficult to define concisely and to understand fully. However, some aspects seem clear. Intuition is more than a guess or a hunch. It is not similar to seeing a strange license plate number and playing it in the state lottery. Intuition is somehow a consequence of an ability to bring, largely subconsciously, a diversity of information and experience to bear on a problem, even though the experience is not necessarily closely related to that problem. Intuitive scientists have a good sense of how nature must work and can often rule out one hypothesis and support another on the basis of this somewhat mysterious sense.

Of course, science cannot progress solely on the basis of intuition. That is precisely where early natural philosophers went wrong. Observations are critical and indispensable. In modern science all hypotheses must be tested objectively against observations. That is the firm foundation on which modern science is based and to which it owes its phenomenal success.

Nevertheless, those with the gift of intuition can often use it to great advantage. They can channel efforts into productive directions and avoid wasteful, unproductive ones. They can bypass steps of minor importance to focus on those of major consequence. Intuition is a valuable asset. It is a component of the subjective side of science being discussed in this book. Those who are so gifted should play on that intuition in order to advance earth science more rapidly and to improve their own chances for discovery.

I recall vividly an incident in a class in intermediate-level physics in which I was a student. The young instructor announced that physics had reached the point (it was then the late 1940s) at which intuition was no longer a part of the science. Like aviation, which had done away with seat-of-the-pants flying, physics, he declared, would hitherto be done solely in a rational, carefully prescribed manner. Solutions to equations would be sought in an orderly fashion; observations would be made in a systematic, methodical manner. This statement came as a disappointment and a blow to those students in the class who were already struck by the adventure of science and who thought they were developing an intuitive sense for how nature works as part of their education. Many of us were ex-servicemen seeking a new way of life. We did not want careers in a field where every step was cut and dried in military-like fashion. I considered termination of my science career then and there. Happily I chose otherwise. What the professor said was, of course, nonsense, at least with respect to the branches of science that I now know best.

There was, is, and will be a place in science for those who are insightful and inspired, who envision great accomplishments, and whose sixth sense tells how to achieve them. And such scientists will likely be the great achievers.

Science needs the insight of the intuitive desperately. Of course, intuition will sometimes lead a scientist astray, but it will also lead to the breaking of barriers, to escaping from the rut, to the new thrust in a new direction and, hence, must be encouraged.

One might consider the question of whether, as a given branch of science evolves into, through, and past its period of major discovery, intuition might be more important in the early stages and of lesser or vanishing importance as the major discovery phase is passed. That is a matter for historians of science to judge. At present, earth science, which receives most attention in this book, has not passed completely through the phase of major discovery, a point that is obvious because many major aspects and features of the earth remain to be observed. Intuition is unquestionably an important component of modern earth science. Probably that is also true for most, or all, other sciences as well.

Examples of the role of intuition in scientific discovery are innumerable. As is widely known, Einstein's work was strongly based on intuition. Holton's account of Millikan's classic determination of the charge on the electron reveals that Millikan intuitively sensed that the value of the charge was "invariant and indivisible" long before the measurements certified this view. Ewing had a remarkable intuition about the earth and was widely known for his ability to "guess" the correct result of an experiment or observation before it took place.

These few isolated examples cannot do justice to the importance of the role of intuition in the history of science. The subject deserves thorough attention and better exposition. What is known to date, however, should provide ample encouragement for those who like to direct their scientific efforts by subjective "feel," as well as more objective considerations.

A related subjective phenomenon perhaps merits a brief digression at this point. It is the phenomenon of the "hot streak." Hot streaks are best known in sports, but they occur in most other human endeavors as well. During a hot streak, everything goes well. Whatever we attempt comes off successfully. Furthermore, we seem to sense intuitively that we are "in the hot streak" or "on a roll." A scientist, for example, may find that everything he or she has been working on falls together and discovery cascades upon discovery for a brief time. The phenomenon of the hot streak is surely not well understood and the subject is a controversial one.

In sports the hot streak is common. A basketball player, for example, makes a series of shots and brilliant plays without a miss or an error. Some have tried through mathematical analysis to attribute the hot streak to statistical fluctuation in a process inherently chancy. That is one view. I do not agree with this conclusion, largely because it is clear that athletes are able to sense when they are in a hot streak. Somehow the athlete knows that things are going well and that his or her performance level is, and likely will be, high. Teammates and coaches and fans can also recognize that an athlete is hot. Good teams respond by giving the athlete more opportunities during the streak. This phenomenon is so widely known and the feeling so regularly sensed that I am not convinced that the sole basis is statistical fluctuation. Nor do I believe that the individual in the hot streak can foresee that future. Instead it seems that the individual can somehow sense (we do not understand how, so we say it is intuitive) that his body and brain have everything performing properly and hence that performance is and probably will be enhanced. It is a subconscious process like the scientific intuition discussed in this section.

Perhaps it seems farfetched to suggest that science might capitalize on such hot streaks in scientists, but, in fact, that is effectively what is attempted at idea sessions, or brainstorming sessions, or certain types of committee activities. Whether the hot streak phenomenon can be further and more systematically exploited by scientists in their quest for discovery is an interesting issue that I raise here and then pass on for the present.

A lighter side to the application of intuition is the so-called Principle of Minimum Astonishment, which is often mentioned in fun by scientists. It means that when controversy arises in science, the view that agrees best with one's intuitive evaluation of the situation is probably correct. The "principle" is really an admonition to rely on one's intuition. At first this principle seems contrary to the quest for surprising discovery that is the focus of this book, but it is not. The trick is to break with convention, not necessarily with intuition. Most new discoveries are not so much counter to good intuition as they are counter to "conventional wisdom" of the science at the time. Plate tectonics, for example, did not counter intuition so much as it did conventional belief.

So in steering a course through the world of science and making the subjective decisions and judgments that affect that course, use some intuition. Intuition has led to many discoveries in the past and will surely lead to many in the future. How do I know? It's easy. I can feel it in my bones!

Avoid Sidetracking to Trivia

A scientific project often involves complex techniques, fascinating devices, involved procedures, and intricate problems. Once caught in this maelstrom of complexity, the scientist is often tempted to focus on a secondary problem and hence to be drawn away from, and to lose sight of, the basic goal. Perseverance in pursuit of the prime goal of the project is nearly always the proper response to this kind of temptation. The secondary problems are often of trivial importance compared with the basic goal, particularly if the project is well designed initially.

This statement will come as a surprise to some. We all know there is always the possibility that research will open a promising avenue to an important unanticipated discovery. In such a case the scientist should, of course, seize the opportunity. That sort of distraction is appropriate. This guideline focuses on another problem, that of the inexperienced scientist who loses a sense of goal or purpose, drifts off course, and wastes effort on fascinating trivia. The scientist must (1) keep his or her sights on the prime and presumably that most important goal and (2) continually reevaluate new developments and respond so as to ensure that the major thrust is toward that goal. But it is not necessary to follow the prescribed path if a better path to the important goal emerges later.

The seeming contradictions in the outline above might be resolved through an example. Often a scientific project is held up by failure of a piece of equipment. Sometimes the proper response is to repair the instrument, but if that process is cumbersome and unmanageable, a better response may be reconsideration of the entire procedure so as to bypass the trouble spot.

This story is told of Ewing, the renowned geophysicist. The setting was a ship on which he was making seismoacoustic measurements. The marine operation was a complex, costly one involving two ships, and any delays would have seriously hindered the project. The instrumentation included a device that sensed acoustic waves incident upon the ship, amplified the signal, and displayed it on a pen recorder. The information so obtained was vital to the project.

At one point, the electronic amplifier failed, bringing operations to a halt. No replacement was available. It seemed a major setback. When Ewing's attention was drawn to the problem, he quickly sized up the entire situation, not just the problem with the amplifier. He reached into his mouth, removed his chewing gum, and stuck it to the pen. The gum destroyed the dynamic balance that had been designed into the pen. It became sensitive, without the additional parts of the system, to movements of the ship corresponding to the impinging acoustic wave. The makeshift device did the job and little time was lost. A lesser scientist might have brought the operation to a standstill while he took on the challenge of repairing the electronic system or might have rerouted the ship to port for a replacement. It was a classic and split-second example of a scientist who never lost sight of the main goal and improvised as needed to achieve that goal.

Be Competitive, Be a Winner, Be First

SCIENCE is a competitive activity; it is not the place for an individual who shies away from competition. Scientists face tough challenges. On the one hand there is the challenge of man or woman against nature. On the other hand there is fierce competition with other scientists in the race for discovery. A zest for competition is an asset in science as it is in many walks of life. And it is fortunate that science is so competitive, for competition brings forth the best efforts of the individual. It is the outstanding effort that leads to discovery. Even the odd scientist who faces a problem in isolation and with no direct competitors needs a strong desire to succeed and outdo others who have worked on the problem previously. Science favors those with a powerful motivation to excel.

Striving for success is only a part of the story, however. Knowing how to succeed, or win, is another part. The art of winning is not often discussed or written about. It is much like the art of discovery in that regard. In fact, the subjects are similar and overlapping; they both involve routes to success and how to chart and follow them.

The art of winning is perhaps most openly and most often taught in sports, although it applies to many other endeavors as well. The art of winning is something more than simply trying to do one's best. Doing one's best at all times is virtually impossible. Recognition of that fact is a basis for the strategy and demeanor of a winner. Winning requires doing one's best at the critical times. And that in turn entails recognition of those critical times based on the state of the game (or endeavor) and the nature of the opponent's response at those times. In basketball, for example, the winning player controls the tempo of a game by making an exceptional move at a time when the opponent is relaxed or when the competition reaches a certain critical point. That situation is sensed by the winner and overlooked by the loser.

Similar tactics apply in science. In science, the exceptional move may be made at a time when a new type of instrument becomes available, or an advance in one field opens a special opportunity in another, or the attention of the bulk of the scientific community is drawn to one topic and away from yet another that happens to provide a special opportunity.

The knack of winning is transferable from one activity to another. A person is sometimes categorized as a "winner" because he or she tends to succeed independently of the particular kind of activity. The knack for winning can be acquired. Coaches teach it. So do major professors. So do leading scientists. Learn from them. Often the instruction is through example.

I once heard a pseudointellectual in a responsible position at a major university expound on an important new trend in education. No longer, the person claimed, would universities train students to strive for success; that concept had become an anachronism. Instead it was more important that the student learn to become a "good loser," so that when things went wrong the student could weather the storm graciously. What hogwash! The general good of society is not served by having a lot of good losers. It is served by having a lot of "good winners." And university students, who are typically among the more talented members of society, should be taught to succeed and to excel in a wholesome manner so that they can lead the society to better itself.

Being first is important in science. The scientific community does not hide that fact. It makes a great deal of being first; some would say too much. Prizes, medals, and other honors depend more on being first than on doing the most nearly complete and thorough job—and justly so. An idea had independently by one person does not merit as much acclaim as the same idea had first by another. The ethics of science requires that ideas had earlier by others must be properly cited in a scientific paper on that subject. The purpose of such citation is to keep the scientific record straight and also to credit the originator. It may or may not be that honor through awards and credit by citation to originators is overdone in science, but in any case there is good reason for that form of honor. The principal purpose, i.e., to stimulate original thinking, is a valid one. A scientist is expected to respond to the incentives established by peers. Strive to succeed, strive to be first.

The story is told of the scientist who was frustrated by regular rejection of his proposals to a government funding agency. He obtained a copy of a successful proposal by another scientist. He copied it word for word and submitted it under his name, noting the duplication and claiming "If you funded his, you must fund mine because it's identical to his." The proposal was, of course, rejected. The reason? Lack of originality. It pays to be first!

Being first into a new area of research usually opens great opportunity for the scientist. Often during the critical period when a new branch of science is opening up, major advances in understanding can be made with little effort and the crudest of analyses in just a few minutes. Later a comparable advance, if one remains to be made, might require years of effort.

For example, during the mid-1960s, the first model of the moving plates of the earth that could predict spreading and converging rates at plate boundaries was developed. For a brief period thereafter, it was possible to sit down with the model and a map of global seismicity and discover for the first time that the down-dip length of the inclined deep seismic zone beneath island arcs is proportional to the convergence rate. This relationship is a powerful and beautiful piece of information. Yet, once the opportunity appeared, it was evident at a glance, almost before one made a simple graph. To make the discovery, one needed only to be at the right place at the right time. The discovery supplied important confirming evidence for the plate tectonic concept and provided a quantum jump in understanding of tectonics and of island arcs. A comparable discovery may not be made in this subject in spite of years or decades of work during a less fertile era such as the present. It pays to be first. It pays to maneuver, with propriety, into a position where one can be first.

Argue by Analogy

THIS guideline is an exceptionally important one. Innovators and discoverers often seem to reason by analogy. Somehow, either subconsciously or consciously, or through both in combination, they recall patterns elsewhere with sufficient similarity to the problem at hand that they are able to solve the problem or choose an appropriate direction for future study. Intuition, discussed earlier, may in fact operate partly through reasoning by analogy, perhaps mostly subconsciously. For some probing of the unknown, the appropriate analogy may well be the best guideline. It pays to develop the habit of seeking analogies that may be useful. Of course, there is potential danger in an imperfect analogy, so caution is in order, but the advantages of reasoning through analogy easily outweigh the disadvantages.

Analogies may involve huge differences in scale of distance and time and huge disparities in the types of phenomena involved and yet still be useful. Often the value is not the simple and obvious one that the physics, say, of the problem can be scaled mathematically. Sometimes the value is just in visualization of a pattern that prevails elsewhere and that resembles in some tenuous way the situation under study. We are fortunate that nature is built of phenomena with similarities and interrelations that manage to transcend the boundaries of the disciplines into which humans have attempted to subdivide science.

A classic example is the analogy between convection in the earth's huge interior and in a pot of soup on the stove. In the earth, convection is thought to drive the plates of plate tectonics. In the pot, heat causes convective circulation in the soup. Froth collects on top of the soup during the process. In the analogy, the airy froth is like the continents. Continents are made of rocks of low density. Like the froth, continents agglomerate and remain at the surface of this earth, while more dense materials in the convection cell return to depths. This analogy immediately conveys to the listener a simple basis on which to think about the earth. Whether it is better to visualize tomato soup or vegetable soup in this regard is another matter, one that likely strains the analogy a little too far!

At sites of great ocean trenches, sea floor is overridden by an advancing island arc or continent located behind the trench. Eventually the ocean floor is consumed and a collision between continents or between a continent and an island arc can occur. Such a collision is one of the most consequential processes of plate tectonics.

A wide range of analogies can be called into play here. Some see the advancing arc or continent like the blade of a great bulldozer, scraping sediments from the sea floor into a wedge of characteristic structure and deformation. The sedimentary wedge is much like the wedge of dirt that precedes the bulldozer at any ordinary construction job. Some see analogy with the cutting tool of a lathe as the advancing arc slices off parts of the colliding continent. Others scrape snow from the roof of their car at near-freezing temperatures and see patterns of deformation in the snow like those in the wedge of sediments forced onto the continent. Of course, the application of each of these analogies is limited, but to discard them because of those limitations would deprive the scientist of a source of ideas and understanding. And it is comforting to know that a process one is proposing to explain some ancient tectonic event is like processes occurring today, even though the scales are much different.

Other analogies are more closely related in a physical sense than the previous examples are. For example, sound waves traveling laterally in the ocean are confined to the vicinity of a zone at a depth where the velocity increases both above and below the zone. The zone is the so-called SOFAR channel. Waves in it propagate very efficiently to long distances. Analogous zones also exist in the solid earth and in the atmosphere where similar velocity structures occur. In fact, there is even analogy with the propagation of light in optical fibers designed to make the velocity increase with distance from the axis. It was argument by analogy with the wave guide in water that focused attention on the possible existence of the wave guides in the atmosphere and the solid earth.

The pervasiveness of analogy in modern science indicates the value and the leverage from reasoning by analogy. Cultivate it.

Vision, Hypotheses, and Objective Testing

TRAINING of science students commonly stresses the objective approach to science. Students are indoctrinated with the techniques of statistics, precision of measurement, and calibration. The quantitative is said to be better than the qualitative. Students are steeped with the need for supercritical assessment of every scientific paper including their own. The objective is said to be better than the subjective. That is appropriate of course. Every scientist must have that objective style and that critical attitude. But one need not, and should not, be supercritical at all times, only when appropriate. Emphasis on objectivity may be so great during training that the young scientist loses sight of the importance, or even the existence, of the sparkling, adventuresome, subjective side of science.

Science often proceeds by the proposing of hypotheses and the testing of those hypotheses against facts, i.e., observattions. The testing must be done objectively and the observations must be carefully scrutinized to ensure that they are, indeed, facts.

The hypothesis need not, however, have a strong basis, or any basis, in fact or observation. It can originate from any source and in any manner. Hypotheses have occurred in dreams. They may be a product of wild imagination, seemingly ridiculous analogy, or sober contemplation. They are a product of the vision of the hypothesizer. Such speculation, dreaming, and vision are an important component of science. The discoverer must use them in order to break out of the mold. Scientists who are timid about proposing a fresh new hypothesis because the evidence has not forced them to do so are not likely to achieve the big discovery.

Of course, each hypothesis must be tested against the facts, all the facts, in the most cold-blooded, unemotional, unbiased, objective fashion. That is the essence of science. Any hypotheses obviously in conflict with the facts should be abandoned with dispatch. Some may be discarded almost instantaneously. But the vitality of science is critically dependent upon the visionary hypothesis, and the potential discoverer must participate in and stress this freewheeling aspect of science.

There is, unfortunately, a tendency on the part of some to attach a stigma to the proposing of a hypothesis that fails. Such an attitude is detrimental to science. Someone who proposes a hypothesis that remains viable and stimulating for some time has done a valuable service for science, even if the hypothesis is eventually discarded. Holding to a hypothesis long after all testing and good judgment have demonstrated that it is incorrect is deserving of some disapproval, perhaps, but proposing a hypothesis and attempting to establish it before definitive testing with negative results is not.

Science would be better served by more consistent encouragement of the imaginative hypothesis than is found in some scientific circles today. There should be sessions at scientific meetings designed to give the bold hypothesizer an opportunity to be heard. There should be forums in the scientific literature for publication and discussion of the unusual hypothesis. Those who cry, "Don't encourage the lunatic fringe!" should be restrained by the recognition that many great advances in science initially seemed part of the "lunatic fringe."

That the stigma on imaginative hypotheses exists is suggested by the professional records of some scientists as they grow older. On attaining senior status, or tenured status, or on nearing retirement, some unexpectedly produce an unconventional hypothesis. While this phenomenon might be attributed to other effects such as the "last gasp," senility, or a tendency to broaden and philosophize with age, I think it likely that some are a consequence of escaping the deleterious effects of the stigma. The secure scientist, or the near retiree, feels free to be more imaginative publicly than the younger counterpart. The secure scientist has established a career and stands to lose little if the hypothesis is wrong. If this phenomenon does occur in science, it is a bad sign, for it suggests that the vision of young scientists is being inhibited. The imagination of younger scientists, and all scientists, should be played upon in order to develop stimulating new hypotheses that can be communicated, debated, tested, and accepted or rejected by the science. Science is not well served by procedures that inhibit vision by scientists of any age group. Nor should science restrict or contain itself by mindless adherence to a rigid interpretation of the so-called scientific method. Science does not progress simply through the "method" in which first a hypothesis is proposed and then the hypothesis is tested by means of evidence assembled for the purpose. Often, as is noted repeatedly in this book, the best procedure is to collect the evidence first by exploring a new frontier. New observations are commonly the stimulant for the hypothesis. Data gathering and hypothesizing, in other words, are appropriate in any order. To insist on a particular order or a rigid style is to constrain the advance of science for no good reason.

The Strategy of Exploration for Understanding

THE term *exploration* is encountered often in science, especially in earth science, where it is commonly used to refer to the search for oil, mineral deposits, or some other particular feature of value. That is not the sense in which the term is used in this guideline. Here it refers instead to the probing of a particular frontier solely for the purpose of developing an understanding of that frontier.

Given an unexplored frontier in science, how should the exploration of it proceed? Should each successive spatial segment of the frontier be explored in great detail, and in order, so that eventually, piece by piece, the entire frontier area will be known? Or should the early stages of exploration be devoted primarily to reconnaissance surveys that attempt to rough out the entire story, to develop the big picture, and to reveal the overall context? Such a procedure would leave the details of each particular segment to be probed later, presumably as an element in that great context.

These two styles, detailed step-by-step exploration and reconnaissance-style exploration, are the extremes. Any exploration program, in fact, is likely to include both styles. But the extremes define a clear-cut difference in strategy. And the sharp contrast and distinct difference emphasize the need to consider this matter in planning the scientific exploration program for a new frontier, for emphasis on one style or the other may hasten or hinder the process of discovery.

In exploring an unknown feature, the appropriate first step is to make reconnaissance surveys and develop a basic understanding of the feature. This procedure will avoid the wasting of effort on detailed surveys of small elements that have little importance in the overall scheme. Before the development of the basic overall understanding, the value of a detailed survey of a small element can only be guessed at. Such guesses are often wrong and so the effort to explore those elements in detail is misspent.

The history of exploration demonstrates the worth of early reconnaissance time and time again. Although he did not consciously plan for it, Columbus discovered America in what amounted to a reconnaissance-style sweep through an unknown part of the earth. The journeys of Magellan, Cook, Tasman, Lewis and Clark, and many other geographical explorers are examples of exploration in similar style. In planetary science, reconnaissance surveys are the obvious first step before detailed exploration of a particular planetary or lunar site. Reconnaissance-style surveys clearly seem to merit priorities in the early stages of exploration.

Where and what then is the problem? The problem is partly that the unknown great frontier may not be recognized as such. Proposers of new science projects therefore ignore the big opportunity and cautiously probe in detail the next obvious small element of the frontier. The problem also arises partly because of strong indoctrination of scientists in the need to probe deeper and deeper into a subject. Now there is nothing wrong with the drive to explore and understand in depth. But frontiers may have both depth and breadth. At certain times insistence on exploration of a limited feature in depth may delay understanding of the broader context of the feature and hence the feature itself.

Consider the exploration of the ocean basins during the period immediately after World War II as an example. Little was known of the sea floor at that time. The few previous oceanographic expeditions with their sporadic lead line soundings had not satisfied the need for overall reconnaissance surveys. The ocean basins had to be explored. The question was how to go about it. In particular, what strategy for acquiring information should be followed?

The post–World War II explorers fell into two categories. Some charted lengthy cruises that spanned the world's oceans. They saw all the ocean basins as a single frontier and sought reconnaissance information on the entire frontier. Others, perhaps awed by the apparent magnitude of global surveys, and perhaps more secure in detailed exploration of the more familiar, opposed the long cruises to the deep seas. They did not view the comprehension of the entire ocean basins and their history as a goal that was attainable in their lifetimes. They saw the overall task as one to be accomplished piece by piece. They chose to explore the near-shore areas in detail first. If their motivation had been solely exploration for recoverable resources, emphasis on study of the margins might have made sense. But their motivation was simply a compulsion to solve all nearby problems before stepping farther. They felt, for example, that detailed understanding of the submarine canyons of the continental margin was an appropriate prime goal. Of course, those canyons are interesting features and worthy of study, but they are of secondary importance in science compared with the ocean basins themselves.

History showed unequivocally, of course, that the reconnaissance school was correct. The great sea voyages produced the observations that led to the discovery of plate tectonics and a fundamental understanding of the nature of the ocean basins. Almost all features of the sea floor, including the canyons, which are but one component of a drainage system that involves deep basins as well, became better understood in the process.

A strict parallel to the post–WWII exploration of the ocean basins can be found in modern exploration of the buried continental crust. The continental crust is a, perhaps the, great frontier of modern earth science. It is huge in volume, full of information, and largely unexplored. And various techniques are in hand for exploring the buried crust.

In this situation it seems obvious that great new discoveries will result from reconnaissance surveys of the crusts of the continents. Like the ocean basins, the continents are so large that they must be of fundamental importance in global geology. It would be one of the most anomalous episodes in the history of exploration of the earth if major discoveries were not revealed as three-dimensional information on continental geology is obtained. We should, it seems, get on with the reconnaissance surveying of the crust of all the continents as expeditiously as possible so as to reap the benefits of the discoveries for society.

But the reconnaissance style is opposed by those with a different strategy. Or perhaps it is no strategy at all. They believe that each newly discovered feature should be explored in great thoroughness by all available techniques *before* moving on to the next feature. The rationale for this position cannot be based on optimization of scientific discovery. The lessons of history seem clearly in favor of early reconnaissance surveying if major scientific discovery is the only goal. Some other motive must be called upon to justify the view that detailed multidisciplinary studies of next-step sites are most appropriate at this time.

THREE

Tactics for Discovery

IN contrast to the term "strategy," which refers to large-scale activity and long-term policy, "tactics" refers to short-term, small-scale activity and action. Those military terms do not translate precisely to classification of activities in science. Nevertheless, "tactics" is used in the title of this chapter, which presents guidelines of more immediate application than those in the preceding chapter on strategy.

Adapt and Adopt Instruments and Techniques

THIS guideline describes what is probably the most consistently successful way to make new discoveries in an observation-oriented branch of science. Everyone should know it. The trick is simply to bring instruments and measurement techniques from one branch of science into a different branch for the first time. Scientists have often made discoveries about the earth by adopting a measurement technique of, say, physics and applying it to a problem in earth science. In such cases, the essential contribution of the discoverer is the recognition of the problem and of the capability of the technique to provide observations critical to its solution. It is not invention of the technique, even though considerable development may be required to adapt the technique to the new problem.

This approach to science is so effective because new kinds of observations of an important scientific phenomenon nearly always produce surprise and discovery. Thus finding and recognizing the technique that will produce the new kind of observation is the key to discovery.

There are innumerable examples of success by those who have followed this pattern. For example, the mass spectrometer is a device that was first developed by physicists for studying properties, particularly mass, of components of matter. Geochemists quickly recognized the potential importance of such measurements in study of certain problems of the earth. Thus began a long sequence of development and application of the mass spectrometer technique to provide unprecedented information on ages and composition of earth materials. Earth science was changed enormously by this one instrument.

As usual, and as described elsewhere in this book, those who entered the field early were richly rewarded for their efforts. But they had to learn a new technique and contribute to its development, often by building their own versions of the device. Now this kind of activity is often carried out in a more mature manner. A mass spectrometer can be ordered from a catalog and purchased from companies in Japan, Europe, and the United States. Many interesting things in earth science remain to be done through application of the mass spectrometer, but the first blush of excitement and the opportunity to make major advance with minimum effort have faded. Spotting the opportunity early produced special reward.

Optical microscopes, radiation counters, electron microscopes, lasers, precision clocks, and computers are examples of other devices developed for another purpose and eventually made highly productive in earth science.

The flux-gate magnetometer had a more complex history of travel through boundaries of disciplines yet a similar end result. Initially conceived during the 1930s within the petroleum industry for exploring geologic structures through their effect on the earth's magnetic field, the magnetometer was called into service during World War II as a device to detect submerged submarines. This function was so important to the war effort that the device was rapidly developed to more sophisticated levels during this period. After the war, it was used not only by the petroleum industry for its original purpose but also by the academic ocean-ographic institutions for exploration of magnetic anomalies of the sea floor. Eventually the flux-gate magnetometer was largely supplanted by the proton precession magnetometer. Neverthe-less, it was one of two devices that provided the information on the spatial pattern of marine magnetic anomalies that was the key to the discovery of sea floor spreading, a concept that is a basic building block of plate tectonics.

The lesson from these examples, and many others unrecorded here, is clear. To develop a new route to discovery in earth science, learn about and monitor other sciences such as physics, chemis-try, materials science, biology, computer science, and various kinds of engineering. Understand the capability of the new instruments and techniques used in those fields. The developers of those devices are often unaware of opportunities for application in earth science. Use the advantage of a background in earth science to find imag-inative new ways to use those techniques so as to foster discovery in geology. It has often been done before. It will be done again.

Skim the Cream

THIS guideline may surprise the science student who has been taught to "dig deeper" and to pursue science in a careful, meticulous manner. Digging deeper is often meritorious, but it is not the only way to make progress in science. In certain situations, there is a better way to proceed.

Exploration of a new frontier can produce observations in abundance. Faced with a large quantity of fresh observational material, it is often best to put off digging deeply into selected sets of data and to scan the entire set of data casually at first. There may be major discoveries to be found at first glance. Such an approach is what is meant here by the phrase "skimming the cream."

The justification for cream skimming is not only that the great result may be arrived at more easily and quickly but also that the great discovery is likely to cast all subsequent work on that problem and that data set in an entirely new light. Special detailed analyses that dug deep but that preceded the main discovery may well become obsolete. Cream skimming, in other words, can prevent wasted effort, direct new effort in a more profitable and effective manner, and, of course, produce the great result.

In the training of modern scientists, emphasis is often placed on careful, methodical behavior with thorough consideration and examination of each advancing step. Caution and conservatism are espoused. Each step, it is said, should be understood before the next step is undertaken. There is no quarrel here with such indoctrination into science. It is because of such meticulous procedure, testing against fact at every opportunity, and attention to detail that science has its firm basis and foundation for further advance.

In exploring the unknown, however, the most cautious step-by-step procedure may not be the most efficient route to the desired end result, which is the thorough understanding of that facet of science. Instead, the rough reconnaissance style in which the investigator tries to grasp the big picture as early as possible is likely to be superior. Think big, skim the cream, try for the great advance, the paradigm that reorients the science. That is the message of this section.

In the late 1950s, Heezen and Tharp were preparing a physiographic map of a section of the midocean ridge for which new sounding data were available when Marie Tharp noticed that earthquake hypocenters tended to occur beneath a prominent central valley, or rift, of the submarine mountain range. She called this fact to the attention of Ewing and Heezen. They speculated that such a rift must always accompany a seismic belt at sea. They were thus able to use earthquake data to interpolate and extrapolate the existence and location of the great rift system through areas where depth soundings were sparse or nonexistent. They "skimmed the cream" from the meager sounding data and limited earthquake data to arrive at the conclusion that a spectacular rift system, twice the circumference of the earth in length, circled the earth. Subsequent observations showed their conclusion to be correct. An important step in understanding the dynamics of the earth had been taken.

Scientists with lesser goals, or those too heavily indoctrinated in the need to explore every topic in great depth, might have focused all attention on the configuration of the ridge at the few places where thorough soundings were available. They would not have arrived at the grand conclusion of a global rift system that placed subsequent studies of the sea floor in a new light. It was a time to skim the cream or, to use another metaphor, to see the forest instead of the trees.

Those who attempt to skim the cream are often the targets of disdain from more plodding coworkers. Such disdain may endure if the cream skimmer is wrong, but it is sadly and embarrassingly misplaced if he's right. In science, as in baseball, cream skimmers, like home run hitters, strike out occasionally, but home runs win the games and home run hitters get the big salaries and the plaudits of the crowd.

Minimize Jargon

EXCESSIVE use of jargon in science is currently hindering communication among scientists and hence inhibiting syntheses. The essence of this guideline is that minimizing jargon, and otherwise improving scientific communication, would enhance opportunity for discovery by facilitating synthesis.

Science progresses in a variety of ways. At one extreme are specialized analytical studies of great detail but very limited scope. At the other extreme are broad-ranging syntheses that integrate information of great quantity and diversity. The individual investigator must choose the mode that best suits him or her at any particular time. Many factors in the structure of the modern scientific enterprise favor specialization. Few encourage synthesis, many discourage it. For example, compartmentalization of university departments and funding agencies, peer review, the publish-or-perish attitude toward employment and promotion, and the proliferation of specialized journals are all factors tacitly favoring specialization in science and tacitly inhibiting synthesis.

Excessive jargon is yet another factor. It inhibits synthesis partly because the prospective synthesizer must use valuable time to learn a wide variety of jargon and partly because the potential for broad synthesis cannot be recognized because of jargon-built barriers between sciences. Few modern scientists are fluent in the jargon of more than one discipline. No scientist today is fluent in the jargon of all sciences. A scientist in one field may have as much difficulty reading the literature of another scientific field as a layperson does.

There is a place for jargon. It occurs when communication is hopelessly inefficient without it. But even then its use should be held to a bare minimum. There is no justification for jargon in pretense or in isolation of a cognoscenti. Making the subject obscure through excessive jargon is one of the principal evils of professionalism. It seems self-evident that both science and society are better served by making science widely known among scientists and nonscientists. Excessive use of jargon is an important component of the general problem of communication in science today, and as such it is a major obstacle in the race for discovery.

Speak (Listen) to the Earth, and It Shall Teach Thee

THIS particular guideline is taken from the King James version of the Bible (Job 12:8). The admonition is rather well known in earth science. In fact, it is carved into the portal of a building for geological study on the campus of at least one major university (Columbia). It means, as I interpret it, that the best way to learn about the earth is through observation. Careful collection of data and careful study of them are the keys to success in earth science. Those who cultivate the ability to communicate with the earth through observation will learn most about it.

Job's admonition is inspiring and, although written long ago, remains valid in this day of modern science. Observation is the ultimate truth of science. Laws, theories, concepts, hypotheses, or whatever we choose to call them have, at least according to one school of philosophy of science, no significance other than as a means for the organization of observations. When in doubt, modern science says, always turn to the observations for resolution of that doubt. Job, though not a practitioner of modern science, was nevertheless on a modern track.

The history of earth science, and all science, is full of examples illustrating this lesson. During the nineteenth century the Neptunists, for example, attributed many geological features to the action of the Noachian flood. They prevailed in geology in Europe for a time on the basis of scholarly appearances. But they were an "eddy" (see Chapter 2). Eventually they met their demise as geologists were driven to the field to test the hypotheses they were taught. In the language of the day, geologists had to "go and see." Once in the field they quickly made observations that dictated explanations other than the flood, and Neptunism was discredited.

Consider another example. The floors of ocean basins, or parts of them, were once thought to consist of rocks like those of the continents, an idea now known to be false. It was a time when observations of the sea floor were sparse indeed. The idea was discarded when earth scientists spoke to the earth and learned otherwise. In this case "speaking" to the earth involved firing large explosions of TNT that sent seismic waves through the rocks of the ocean floor to return to the surface with evidence of the noncontinental nature of the rocks. Job did not mention the use of TNT, of course, but his message was correct. Observation was the key.

The following story is in part a sad one, so poignant in places for some that it might better be passed over, except that it illustrates, more clearly and more dramatically than any other example I know, the essential and all-powerful role of observation in science. The story concerns Harold Jeffreys, a brilliant British geophysicist who was a dominant figure in the earth sciences for nearly half a century. He was knighted for his exceptional achievements and so became Sir Harold in science. The story is based solely on material available in the literature and not on personal communication or hearsay.

Jeffreys was an outstanding mathematical geophysicist. He brought a rigorous, quantitative, analytical style to a great diversity of scientific problems ranging from the rheology of the earth's interior through nearly every aspect of seismology to the age and thermal history of the earth and the figure of the earth and its moon. Jeffreys was a giant of his time, held in awe, and deservedly so, by most earth scientists throughout much of his career.

He made one step, however, that diminished his stature among his colleagues and that deflected some of the acclaim that might otherwise have been his. When Wegener's ideas of continental drift appeared and were being debated, Jeffreys took a stand against drift and soon became a leader of the opposition. That move, in the eyes of modern earth scientists, was wrong. His position against drift was based on his ideas of the rheology of the earth. The details of the arguments are not important to the story.

Jeffreys continued his opposition to drift and, when plate tectonics appeared, extended it to include opposition to plate tectonics, a position that almost all modern earth scientists also consider to be in error. He did not relent, at least in public, before his death in 1989. In the eyes of many, Jeffreys became the symbol of opposition to plate tectonics. He was attacked, sometimes with less than deserved respect, by rising young aspirants to leadership in the field. He lost prestige within the scientific community to a degree that seems far out of proportion for someone who had otherwise contributed so much to earth science.

And so we come to the key part of the story. How, indeed, could so brilliant a scientist as Jeffreys have misstepped and taken the wrong direction on this most crucial matter? The answer may perhaps be found in his widely known book *The Earth.* He likely went astray partly because he formed an opinion of a matter before adequate observations relevant to the matter were known to him or perhaps even available.

The critical information may be found on pages 289 and 290 of the third edition of *The Earth* published in 1952. At this point of the book he was analyzing the cooling of a model of the solid earth. He recognized that, under certain conditions, some fusion (melting) would occur at depth. The following words then appear in the text:

> There is a complication at this point because we should ordinarily have in this state a solid crust resting on a less dense liquid. As a pure problem in mechanics such a state would be stable if the crust was thick enough, and there is no reason why it should not become permanent. If it was too thin, or if it broke anywhere under some local disturbance, instability would arise and would lead to wholesale fractures of the outer crust. Solid blocks would be continually foundering and melting on the way down, while the fluid would actually come to the surface in places. The thermal balance at the surface would be as follows. The heat supply from the interior would be insufficient in any case to keep a large fraction of the surface fluid; at any moment most of it would be solid, the blocks being separated by veins of fluid.

Jeffreys was clearly on the track of plate tectonics when he wrote those words. From a theoretical study of a cooling earth he had reasoned his way to an earth not identical to but much like the one we visualize when we think of plate tectonics today. Unfortunately just a few lines later he says:

This would be a tempting explanation of surface igneous activity, but unfortunately it requires a continuous connection among the liquid parts at the surface, with the solid blocks separated. Actual igneous activity is always local and the crust has remained connected through geological time.

Those sentences reveal his fatal error.

Remember, it was sometime before 1952 that this work was done. The Mid-Atlantic Ridge was known at that time but only crudely. It was not thought of as the locus of great volcanism. It was not known to be a part of a great globe-encircling rift. And Jeffreys may not have been aware that the geological evidence for intermittent volcanism could, in fact, be interpreted as a manifestation of what might be considered continuous volcanism in a longer term perspective. Lack of observations, or inadequate interpretation of them, led to Jeffreys's downfall in this case. If his theoretical work had been done later when the midocean rift system was better known, or perhaps he had been willing to recant some of his earlier conclusions, Jeffreys might have emerged as a leader—rather than an opponent—of the plate tectonics revolution. Sound and close attention to observation was, once again, the key to progress in science and inadequate observation a roadblock or diversion.

A somewhat similar story from the discipline of seismology illustrates that the preceding is not a unique example. A seismogram of a distant earthquake typically displays two kinds of waves: body waves and surface waves. The body waves, which travel through the earth's interior, are pulselike. The surface waves, which, as the name implies, travel along the surface, are usually oscillatory with durations of many tens of minutes and with a character that is near sinusoidal. For many years this long duration and near-sinusoidal character were enigmatic, and various explanations, mostly incorrect, were proposed. In the 1920s, one seismologist proposed that the effect of the ocean on the traveling surface waves dispersed them to such a degree that they acquired this particular character. He developed an elegant mathematical theory to predict the effect of the water on the waves. It turned out that the wave period in the theory was proportional to water depths, a logical and reasonable result. He then put the average depth of the oceans, 3 km, into the formula and predicted a period of 9 seconds for the sinusoidal seismic wave train. As the observed period is about 15 seconds, he concluded that the discrepancy was so great that the theory must be inappropriate and that the water was not the cause of the observed phenomenon. This conclusion was in error.

It was another case of insufficient attention to observation. If the areas of shallow seas are ignored and only the typical deep ocean areas are considered, the average depth of the oceans is about 5 km or a little more. When this figure is put into the formula, the theory predicts the period of the seismic wave train to be near 15 seconds, as observed. It is indeed the effect of the oceanic water layer that produces that prominent effect on seismic surface waves. It was some twenty years before seismologists more familiar with the bathymetry of the sea floor established this effect and recognized the basic error in use of observation by the early investigator.

Job's admonition in biblical language was once paraphrased, probably unknowingly, by a hard-bitten field geologist. He said, "If the data wanna talk rock, let 'em talk rock!" The meaning was no different. The message seems sufficiently important that it merits more than one style, one for stone over the entrance to a stately campus building, another for voice transmission over a campfire surrounded by crusty observers of the earth.

The story of the discovery of the inner core of the earth is a clear-cut example of the use of careful observation to make and win the case. It is also an inspiring story for young scientists and particularly for young women who aspire to discovery in science.

In the early part of the twentieth century, seismologists were acquiring data from earthquakes in seismic belts throughout the world as recorded at seismograph stations throughout the world. The seismic waves traversed the interior, including the very deepest parts of the earth. From these data, it soon became clear that the earth has a deep nonrigid center, a spherical core that fails to propagate shear waves. The outer surface of the core is located at a depth of about 2900 km, roughly half the radius of the earth which is about 6400 km. The solid mantle overlies the core and is in turn overlain by a thin crust.

During the 1920s and early 1930s, some puzzling waves traversing the deep interior were noticed. After some consideration, they were identified by the leading authorities as a consequence of diffraction associated with propagation through the spherical core, and that explanation became, for a time, the established one.

During the 1930s, a young Danish woman working in seismology began a thorough study of these waves. Her name was Inge Lehmann. After long and careful evaluation of the data, she concluded that the waves were not diffracted. Instead, she claimed, they had traveled through, and been affected by, a hitherto unsuspected inner core of the earth, a body smaller than the main core and embedded in its center. This challenge to the establishment generated controversies, but Inge stuck by her guns, and the guns in this case were the most powerful ones in science, the observations. Eventually she won out, the concept of the inner core was accepted, and modern seismologists continue to accept and refine her model.

Strangely, the story of Inge Lehmann's major contribution to the understanding of the earth's interior is rarely quoted in accounts of important scientific discoveries by women scientists. Perhaps that is because of her innate modesty and aversion to limelight. Her inspirational story deserves more widespread attention and recognition. She knew when the data wanted to talk rock, and she let 'em talk rock.

A variation of the biblical quote from Job has arisen, with no disrespect intended, from the field of earthquake seismology. It says "*Listen* to the earth, and it shall teach thee." This version seems apt for a scientific discipline in which most of the observational effort is based on continuous year-round listening at thousands of seismograph locations throughout the world. The other possible motivation for this change, i.e., humility on the part of seismologists to a degree exceeding that of Job's, seems less likely to this seismologist!

Go for the Spatial Pattern

THIS guideline is a specific tip on how to make important discoveries about the earth. And it can be applied to other subjects as well. The tip is remarkably simple. It deserves mention only because it is frequently overlooked. The trick is to concentrate attention on the spatial pattern—of almost anything.

The spatial pattern of features is often very revealing. It is commonly more revealing than a very precise quantitative model. That is because the model is often an oversimplification of reality. The simple model is in the reductionist style of good physics. It may be illuminating and should not be overlooked. But oversimplifying a part of the earth in order to get a tractable problem may draw attention away from the potent information of the spatial pattern. The earth is not a simple object like an atom or like a block sliding down an incline. It is a complex object, and the spatial pattern of the complexity is often the key to enhanced understanding. In earth science, the classic example of the spatial pattern is the geologic map. The geologic map is probably *the* single most important form of information used in understanding the earth.

Some classroom techniques minimize or bypass the worth of the spatial pattern, perhaps unintentionally. Textbooks usually emphasize quantitative means of analyzing simple examples. Simple examples dominate textbooks. In fact, simple examples are commonly described as "textbook examples"! And textbooks often stress understanding of process and other such matters easily handled analytically. The analysis of spatial patterns is usually more intuitive and less amenable to concise description than straightforward analytical problems are. Hence the spatial patterns receive less emphasis.

But consider the historical record of the use of spatial patterns. The study of magnetic anomalies at sea is an obvious and classic example. The spatial pattern of magnetic anomalies was the key to one of the greatest discoveries of geology, the concept of sea floor spreading. When the first comprehensive measurements of marine magnetic anomalies were becoming available, I was a graduate student in seismology sharing an office with another student working in magnetics. He was bright, energetic, and inexperienced. He tried hard to unravel the mystery of magnetic anomalies at sea. He did what the textbooks implied should be done. He attempted to understand selected anomalies quantitatively by using block models of rocks of different magnetic properties. His efforts revealed little of significance. I secretly congratulated myself for choosing a productive subject like seismology over an unproductive one like magnetics at sea. That was a major error in judgment on my part. Seismology was a good field alright, but magnetics was about to become a spectacular one. As more magnetic data became available, it became possible to map the spatial pattern of the anomalies. The unique striped pattern that evolved was the prime basis for the discovery of the concept of sea floor spreading. The magnetic anomaly pattern can now be used to describe the age of the ocean floor wherever it exists! The pattern is used in a qualitative way. The quantitative explanation is still somewhat enigmatic. This magnificent contribution to earth science based on the spatial pattern of magnetism overshadows by far all other results based on characteristics of the magnetic data other than the spatial pattern.

In the face of the overwhelming evidence for the spatial pattern as the key to discovery in certain subjects, it is surprising that this form of evidence is not more emphasized in other subjects. Consider mineralogy, for example, which has been developed to a very sophisticated level by generations of talented scientists. They have done a magnificent job. A great variety of information is available for almost any particular mineral. But strangely, for most minerals, there is no map of mineral occurrences on a continent-wide scale, i.e., a scale that would be especially valuable for relating mineral distribution processes with large-scale tectonic patterns or processes.

Of course, there are such maps for the economic deposits of any mineral of value. What is missing is a more nearly comprehensive map showing all known mineral occurrences, i.e., places where minerals have been found whether in economic quantities or not. A great deal of this information is probably already collected and stored in the heads or notebooks of field geologists and rock hounds. What is lacking, and perhaps blocking major discovery on mineral genesis because it is lacking, is merely the compilation of existing information on spatial patterns of mineral occurrences.

As another example, consider the seismological study of rocks near the lower boundary of the continental crust, the boundary referred to as the "Moho." This boundary is typically at a depth of about 40 km beneath the continents. The "Moho" is a concept of long standing in earth science. It has become so widely known

and so established in the thinking of earth scientists that the concept has taken on a rigidity not prescribed by data. Until recently, scientists have been taught, and hence "know," that the Moho has a certain structure and is the same everywhere. If studies of two distinct areas indicate different characteristics for the local Mohos, the first inclination is to discredit one or both studies.

Such inflexible thinking and the downplaying of variations that might fall into a comprehensible spatial pattern may well be hiding an important discovery. Spatial variations in the properties of Moho and its surroundings seem evident from many sets of observations. If so, the pattern of spatial variations is likely the key to the big discovery.

Field geologists have a credo that deserves broad circulation and application. "Map it," they say, "and it will come out alright." That expression is another way of stating that the spatial pattern of some property is often the key to discovery.

How to Choose a Graduate School

CHOOSING a graduate school is one of the most important steps in the career of a scientist. For a student aspiring to major discovery, the choice is especially critical. In my view, such a student should choose the school that has the scientist who is the leader in the specialty the student has elected to follow. Not *a* leader, *the* leader. Try to study with the very best.

Determining just who *the* leader in a field may be is easier said than done. However, by seeking the advice of faculty members at your undergraduate college and of scientists encountered at meetings and by reading the scientific literature, the basis for a sound decision can be acquired. Once one, or a few, possible mentors have been selected, take the next step well before the deadline for application for admission.

Write to and meet with proposed mentors. Tell each why you are interested in working with him or her. The mentor will be flattered, and you will demonstrate some knowledge of the field and some careful thought. Try to make definite arrangements to work with the chosen person before, or just after, you arrive at the selected school.

The reason for so much emphasis on choice of a major professor is that the way to do scientific research is mostly learned from the mentor. (I know this book is designed for that purpose but it is not a substitute for prolonged personal contact. There is still more to learn!) The overall curriculum, in graduate school, is less critical. Most research-oriented universities provide adequate basic courses in science and mathematics. And anyway it never has been certain that *the* best university overall will teach *the* best course in, say, differential equations, at the time you take it. What is most important in graduate school is to be closely associated with the leader of the field. Only through close association is it possible to learn how he or she thinks, plans, and operates in order to reach and maintain that position of leadership.

As noted in the preface, a quirk of fate caused me, in 1947, to become a graduate student under the direction of Professor Maurice Ewing of Columbia, a truly exceptional earth scientist and leader who, in 1949, founded the Lamont-Doherty Geological Observatory. In those early days, Ewing's graduate students numbered about a dozen. It was an organization that was loosely coordinated but nevertheless full of camaraderie and good-natured rivalry. Incredibly, almost every member of that group went on to a career of distinction in science. They became professors at major universities, presidents of companies, leading scientists in industry and government, directors of institutes, authors, deans, presidents of scientific societies, members of the National Academy of Sciences, and winners of innumerable awards. Many have served in government advisory circles. One, Frank Press, became science adviser to President Carter and then president of the National Academy of Sciences. Another, Charles Drake, currently serves on the Science Council of President Bush.

The members of the group are all blessed with talent, of course, but it is not reasonable to account for their consistent success as a consequence of an accident of fate that assembled a select group, all of whose members were exceptionally talented. Instead it seems more likely that the members all acquired a style and a spirit of success from Ewing and used that style and spirit advantageously in their careers. In this case, study under a great leader was an important factor in many successful careers.

Similar cases from other disciplines may be cited. Rutherford, for example, the great particle physicist of Cambridge University, turned out many students who became widely known in science.

Like many other pieces of advice this one needs to be qualified, and some caution is wise. An occasional great scientist is eccentric to the point of avoiding any interaction with students. And some highly rated ones have already moved beyond their major discovery period to other activities. Some may not be properly rated. Nevertheless, the matter is crucial. A student with only modest talents can be inspired and boosted to important achievement by association with the right leader. And, of course, in turn a leader will flourish through association with good students.

At the undergraduate level the choice of a school is not so critical for a science student so far as basic training in science is concerned. It is not necessary to attend the school that has *the* best undergraduate program in the discipline of interest. It is only necessary to attend a school with a strong undergraduate curriculum in basic science and with sufficient reputation in science so that it will be recognized as such by the graduate school's admissions committee. A well-rounded education in addition to training in science is of great value. And the spirit that pervades a particular school may have an influence on one's career.

Through personal experience, I can cite an example, this one not from science but from athletics. As a student in Massillon, Ohio, I was fortunate to play football under a young coach of exceptional ability. He was no ordinary coach and no ordinary human being. He would become a major figure in professional football. His name was, and is, Paul Brown. Brown was a winner —as a coach at Washington High School, at Ohio State, and with the Cleveland Browns and Cincinnati Bengals, two professional teams that he founded as well as coached. Brown's principles, his spirit, and his innovative strategy rubbed off onto his players, even the mediocre ones like me. He developed some great athletes, of course, from those who were blessed with sufficient talent. What is perhaps more interesting for this discussion is that he also developed a new school of coaching and produced many coaches, some of whom make up a significant fraction of the best coaches of the present era. Furthermore, his impact was not limited to the sports arena. In high school Brown's achievements and his influence spread success throughout the school as debaters, scholars, actresses, and musicians, as well as athletes, were inspired by him to strive for success and, in fact, to achieve that success. Classmates of mine from that era who have been successful in various walks of life often refer to the "winning spirit" that Brown instilled not only in the school but also in the entire town. It was and is a clear-cut case of inspiration by one leader and subsequent achievement by those he inspired. Association with such an inspiring leader is a valuable experience and one to be sought.

Some students complete their undergraduate training without deciding on a specialty for graduate study. Such students should go to a university of quality and breadth in their discipline in order to obtain a master's degree. Once the specialty is decided upon, the student should follow the advice outlined above. For the Ph.D., he or she should go where the leader of that specialty is located, even if it means transferring after the master's degree is granted.

One justification for this advice is that a few leaders seem to turn out disproportionately large numbers of young leaders. Furthermore, it is often recognized by employers that study with outstanding leaders is a valuable asset. It you have done so, make sure that information is on your résumé.

The advice of this section refers solely, of course, to the training phase of an individual's career. At a later stage, the scientist who is bent upon discovery and who is ready to establish new directions in the science, his or her own directions, may well choose an environment not dominated by a leading figure in the science, unless, of course, that leader encourages new initiatives by younger colleagues.

Skim the Rest of the Volume, Any Volume

THIS guideline describes a procedure that can enhance serendipity. The specific procedure is not so important as the attitude illustrated by the example.

Scientists often read and reference papers in volumes of scientific journals of past years. If you have taken the trouble to retrieve such an old volume, do not just read the paper of interest and then return the volume to the library shelf. Instead take a little extra time and skim the rest of the papers in the volume.

Not much effort is involved. If you are lucky you will hit upon something that has grown in significance or interest since it was first published and then filed away.

Old scientific literature is rarely searched thoroughly. In fact, it is rarely searched casually. Most old literature that is read is read because it is part of a reference chain. Even current literature, which at present appears in great volume and rarely in easy-to-read style, is often not well read. Hence, by skimming volumes that you happen to have in hand for another purpose, you may, effortlessly and serendipitously, acquaint yourself with something that is worthwhile and that has escaped the attention of your contemporaries. It is an easy way to find a means to break away from the crowd.

Or, in a slight variation, when you return a volume that you have been reading to its place on the library shelf, skim some of the adjoining or nearby volumes. Once, while operating in this mode, I chanced upon the now famous paper by F. B. Taylor that proposed large lateral movement of the continents well before Wegener's presentation of his hypothesis of continental drift. Taylor's ideas, presented in 1910, were not so well worked out as Wegener's, and they did not have the impact on the science community that Wegener's ideas had. Nevertheless, Taylor was on the track of continental drift earlier than Wegener and has become widely recognized for that reason.

When I came across that well-known paper, well known that is after the 1960s, I had never before read it and was pleased to have the opportunity to do so. I was eager to open the book. The paper was printed at a time when it was left to the reader to slit the pages so they could be separated and turned. To my astonishment, the pages of that famous paper had never been slit! That paper, which contained an idea of historic importance to earth science, had rested on the shelves of a library of a major university for more than sixty years without being read! One cannot fault a particular library or its readership for that omission. Innumerable similar situations have occurred elsewhere and must be occurring today. Books on library shelves are a source of old, forgotten ideas and a stimulation for new ones.

Of course, it is also possible, though more time consuming, to skim old literature in a more systematic way. Just go to the library and start with volume one of your favorite journal. Read or skim as far as you can. I once read or skimmed the entire *Bulletin of the Seismological Society of America* in this manner. It was a very educational exercise, far more enlightening than reading the latest textbook on seismology. It revealed how ideas, techniques, and seismologists appeared and evolved, and it was a source of ideas that shaped future research projects. To do the same for that journal now, as opposed to when I was a student, is a much more formidable task as a result of proliferation of papers and scientists. Nevertheless, skimming the old literature is an experience different from a computer search for papers on a particular topic. It may provide the skimmer with just the edge necessary to be first with a particular discovery.

Do It Yourself

ONE characteristic of modern science already noted is the strong channeling of projects and individuals toward specialization. This effect is a blessing and a curse. Penetrating, esoteric tasks demand full-time specialized effort. But there is also a place and a need for the versatile, well-rounded scientist who, in addition to a specialty, has a background of understanding in a variety of techniques and skills, scientific and nonscientific. Students of science can enhance their opportunities in science, their understanding of the world, and their skills by doing a wide variety of things for themselves.

The style of learning by doing was, and is, particularly prevalent in study of experimental physics at many universities. Students are expected to design and build instruments, to feel at home in machine shops or electronic shops, and to learn to operate a wide variety of equipment. A similar attitude holds in some other fields but probably to a lesser extent than in physics. The effect of such training shows. Some years ago, a dean at another university related to me that his college had just added two new faculty members, one a theoretician, the other an instrument designer. The instrument designer had a Ph.D. in physics, the theoretician a Ph.D. in mechanical engineering!

A student, or scientist at any level, can enhance competence in science by learning how to run a lathe or milling machine; how to weld or braze; how to design, build, and repair electronic devices; how to run a crane or a bulldozer; how to fly a plane; or any one, or as many as possible, of a thousand skills. The way to learn about the real world is by "doing it yourself." Science students should seize every such opportunity. They have a great advantage over a skilled artisan because they can quickly grasp the scientific principles behind a particular process.

During World War II there was a grand shake-up of society. Young people, men mostly, who would eventually make careers in science were led or forced into other activities as part of the war effort. They were made into tank and truck drivers, radar repairmen, weather forecasters, navigators, demolition experts, automobile mechanics, cooks, plumbers, and sonar technicians. In the postwar period, ex-servicemen with such experience became a major part of the population of science students. It was a very fertile time in science as the diverse skills of this group were drawn upon in scientific activities. They had "done it themselves" and they came to science with something special to contribute.

For the modern student caught in the track of formal education in science, it is difficult to escape from the limited sphere of the classroom and laboratory so as to become acquainted with the way the rest of the world functions. Nevertheless, when opportunity arises, the science student should move so as to learn a variety of skills, to become familiar with a broad range of subjects, and to participate in a diversity of activities. Breadth, like depth, is an asset.

The Knack of the Fresh Perspective

To achieve success in research, it is important to maintain an appropriate perspective of one's own work.

It is remarkably easy to allow one's perspective to shrink so that the problem in question is seen only very narrowly. Everyone, it seems, suffers from this difficulty. Yet it is quite possible, and it is not difficult, to force oneself to view any problem from different perspectives. Often a new perspective is the key to discovery. This guideline calls for conscious effort to see the problem at hand, whatever it may be, in a new light, even a variety of lights.

For example, consider the matter of scale. In most scientific endeavors, or almost any activity for that matter, we tend to become trapped, subconsciously, into thinking at a certain scale. The geologist searching for hydrocarbons thinks on the scale of an oil field. The petrographer at the microscope thinks on the scale of a thin section. The field mapper thinks on the scale of a quadrangle, an outcrop, or a day's journey. The geophysicist may think on the scale of the entire earth; the cosmologist, on the scale of the universe.

An important trick in research is to force oneself to think of the same problem but from a perspective of different scale. The petroleum geologist may profit by seeing not just the oil field but the entire sedimentary basin that holds the oil field in the grander context of collision of continents and spreading of oceans. The petrographer may look for patterns of change in the microscopic features that show consistent correlation over continental dimensions, not just the scale of an outcrop or the scale of a mineral deposit. The geophysicist may drop to the scale of a specimen in a laboratory press in an effort to understand the mechanics of phenomena of global scale.

In retrospect, the valuable new perspective often seems an obvious choice, yet also in retrospect many such obvious choices seem long overlooked.

Who can forget Carl Sagan's delightful account of the imaginary giant in space who watched the earth for billions of years and saw nothing of interest. Then, after a near eternity of waiting, a tiny rocket left the surface and entered space briefly, only to fall back to earth in just a few minutes. After a few more years another rocket rose to place a grapefruit-size body in orbit. And so on to present and future space travel. It was a clever description that let us see our own activities in a fresh new light and from the perspective of the earth's multibillion-year history.

The case of the earthquake focal mechanisms provides an example of the advantage of a change in perspective. Earthquake focal mechanism studies reveal the orientation of the plane of rupture in the earth and the directions of movement of rocks on opposite sides of that fault plane. The initial studies of earthquake focal mechanisms were made in Japan and based on data from seismographs and observations of land movement in a limited area of Japan. The studies were directed to only local seismic zones and local earthquakes. Related phenomena elsewhere were excluded. Eventually similar studies followed for local events in other parts of the world. But for some time, the perspective of the phenomenon was kept on a local scale. Then it was suggested that there might be a consistent global pattern to such movements. And there was. The global pattern of focal mechanisms became a strong piece of evidence in support of the concept of plate tectonics. Most of the large earthquakes, it turned out, occurred at plate boundaries and corresponded to the relative movement of adjoining plates. What began as a study of an isoated earthquake and a phenomenon of local scale evolved to a study of global scale and significance as the perspective changed.

Choose Your Problem Very Carefully

PERHAPS the most important decision that a scientist in basic research makes is the choice of the problem on which to work. Choose a problem that is trivial, and the result will be trivial. Choose a problem that is intractable or beyond the capability of the investigator, and the result may be years of frustration and little accomplishment. Choose a problem that everyone else is working on, and the result may be no more distinguished than that of an ordinary voice in a community sing. A wise choice of problem is a critical matter in the career of a scientist.

Some scientists make this choice rather casually. A scientist may work on a particular problem just because it happened to be the first one to come to mind when it was time for a new effort to begin. Or perhaps the problem was chosen because a professor chanced to mention it in class. Or perhaps it was chosen because an acquaintance was working on a related matter. Sometimes a scientist will spend only a few minutes thinking about what problem to attack and then spend months or years working on the problem. All of the foregoing are weak bases for choice of an activity that may consume a substantial fraction of a scientist's life.

A scientist should give very careful deliberation to the choice of the problem, spending considerable time on it if required. A scientist should select a problem (1) whose solution will be important to the flow of the science and (2) that is capable of being solved by someone with the particular talent, experience, and capacity of that individual.

Many young scientists make the error of choosing a problem of little or, at best, modest significance because they feel that such a problem will fall within their range of capabilities. This course is often an incorrect one. Significance does not necessarily correlate with difficulty. Problems of major significance are often as easy or easier to solve than many problems of trivial significance.

In selecting a problem for a basic research project (1) spend some time and think very hard about the matter, (2) do not settle for what happens to be at hand, and (3) choose the most fundamental and most significant problem that may yield to your capabilities and endeavor.

Once the decision is made, there should follow an exploratory period during which the means of attacking and solving the problem are investigated. Typically this is done by examining critical data. One might want to ascertain, for example, that there is a real effect that can be well documented by data, not just a supposed one. There may, in fact, be no evidence for the supposed effect. Or, conversely, it may be that the very first perusal of the data, if done intently, will produce the major discovery. If the former, the project should probably be dropped and the procedure to select a new problem begun again. If the latter, the game is already won and the scientist needs only to flesh out the observations and make the case in a formal way. The first stage of preliminary investigation is often crucial in one way or another, and the scientist should be prepared to change course abruptly if the early investigation so dictates. So try hard to pick a winner. If you make a poor choice, drop that problem as gracefully as possible and pick another. There is no point in lackluster plodding in a hopeless cause just because of reluctance to admit an early error of judgment.

There is no need here to cite examples of choices of research problems of little significance. They can readily be found on the shelves of the library. Just look through any scientific journal. There will be many papers in it that represent a great deal of effort by the author and that are extremely well done but that are, nevertheless, ignored by the bulk of the scientific community. Few will ever care that such a paper was written. What is wrong? It is obvious. The problem chosen had little significance. The solution attracts no attention. The paper is not referenced or mentioned. No one does anything different as a consequence of the paper. Yet the author did a competent, creditable job but made just one error—working on a trivial problem.

On the other hand, there are also many examples where a modest amount of work produced a paper of great consequence. The brilliance was in the choice of the problem and the approach to the problem, not in the intricacies of the method of solving the problem. Vine and Matthews's paper on the magnetic anomalies associated with the spreading sea floor is an example. The problem was extremely important, the perception of the situation outstanding, and the method ingenious, but the solution is so simple and straightforward that it can be described and sketched in a few minutes and anyone can readily understand it.

University faculties and research laboratories are commonly populated by talented scientists of great potential who have attained their position through some early, clever achievement but who have never fulfilled that potential and promise. Often their only shortcoming is failure to select an appropriate research area, one of significance beyond that of routine science. Put to work on a problem of importance on either their own initiative or that of their employer, they might achieve distinction. Lacking that initiative they may become forever mundane.

The Curve of Discovery

IN exploring any particular subject, or any particular frontier, a pattern of discovery often evolves that is consistent from one subject to another. The consistency is so obvious that it is evident even in the face of inadequate means to measure discovery quantitatively. If one plots cumulative knowledge as a function of time using almost any measure of knowledge, the curve will rise slowly at early times, then rise rapidly during a relatively short interval, then flatten out to become asymptotic to the total quantity of knowledge available in that subject. There is, in other words, an interval of slow learning, followed by a period of rapid discovery, followed by a period of greater knowledge but, once again, a slow increase in knowledge.

The geographical exploration of the earth's surface in a global sense provides an excellent example. To simplify the example, consider only knowledge of geography assembled so that a single individual can comprehend it. Ignore, in other words, the uncommunicated knowledge of a primitive society. In this subject there was an interval of millions of years during which humans slowly added knowledge about their surroundings but none knew about more than a fraction of a single continent. Then about five hundred years ago the interval of great discovery began. Humans began to explore the entire globe and to transmit the acquired knowledge broadly. Huge features, including seas, continents, and island chains, were discovered in rapid succession. The entire surface of the earth can now be comprehended. But now the period of discovery is over. There is nothing left to discover. Such a pattern is often repeated as humans explore other aspects of their surroundings.

The would-be discoverer can help the cause by trying to ascertain the current position of the specialty relative to the rapid-discovery portion of the curve. That is easier said than done, for the position on the curve cannot be known for sure at that time. However, recognition that such a curve typically is followed can be used to gain an edge by a discoverer. Try to analyze the position of your specialty at the present. If discovery seems on the rise, stick with it. If discovery is on the wane, examine the matter carefully to ascertain whether the cause is inadequate effort by scientists or simply exhaustion of possibilities for discovery. If it seems to be the latter, and you are discovery bound, look at alternate specialties.

Availability of significant observations can be used as a measure of position on the discovery curve. An abundance of unexplained observations or opportunities to make important new observations are indications that the discovery curve has not yet flattened. Judging whether a given set of observations is significant or important is not always easy. Sometimes, however, the decision is obvious simply because of the large scale or broad scope of the feature under study or because of its role in a larger context.

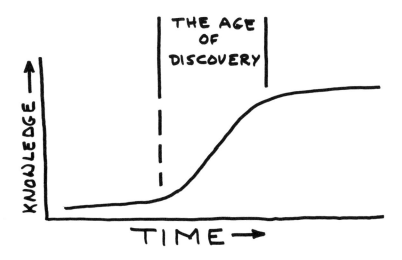

Overcoming the "Terminal Paper"

As every scientist knows, science does not advance with the steady and orderly progress that is sometimes implied in media accounts of science for the nonscientist. Science is beset by fads, abrupt changes in direction, growth and decay of interest in a particular subject, mundane activity, and sparkling, exciting, creative activity. The course, in fact, often seems helter-skelter, but it is not completely so. Patterns of change from one style of activity to another are sometimes repeated and sometimes recognizable as repeating patterns. The scientist who first recognizes such a pattern of change as it is occurring may be able to forecast the next development and so be positioned advantageously for the next discovery. This guideline concerns one particular pattern that can sometimes be detected and that may portend opportunity for discovery.

In previous sections of this book there are discussions of certain phases in the development of a branch of science. The observational phase provides new data on previously unexplored features or phenomena. In the discovery phase, the new observations are used to reveal new understanding of nature. Often during the "discovery" phase, the new revelations are cast in raw and crude form. The "do-it-right" phase follows as raw discoveries are tidied up, puzzles are solved, theory is made elegant, and the entire subject couched in sophisticated language.

Sometimes this sequence of events leads to one grand piece of work, a synthesis of all previous study woven together in elaborate, elegant, and sophisticated form. Often a part of the grand paper is mathematical, written crisply and concisely in obscure mathematical style so that it can be read only with substantial effort and so that it defies casual skimming. I do not mean to be critical of such contributions. They may be monumental. They are usually very well done by the best of scientists and represent a major positive contribution to science.

Such papers are what I refer to here as "terminal" papers. They are so good and so comprehensive that they give the impression that the subject is mastered and hence discourage further work in that field. Established scientists tend to move their efforts elsewhere, prospective new entrants to the field are deterred, and the field, whether it be fertile or infertile, lies fallow for a long interval.

But often the "terminal" paper is not so comprehensive as it first appears. There may be much left to discover in that field. The magnificent terminal paper may mask significant opportunity. In such a situation, with opportunities overlooked by others, competition in the field of the terminal paper may be minimal and the would-be discoverer may find clear sailing to an important advance. To discover, try to find a field in which opportunity has been hidden by a terminal paper and jump into it before the opportunity is recognized by others. Here is an example of such a field and such a possible opportunity in my discipline, seismology.

Seismographs are operated at thousands of locations throughout the world for monitoring earthquake activity. The sensitivity of the instruments is such that they record ground motion continuously. Earthquake-generated motion predominates during only a small fraction of the time. At all times, however, the seismographs record a background noise called microseisms. An overwhelming proportion of the seismological data collected concerns microseisms, not earthquakes. The microseism noise varies with time in very complex fashion. It is known to have numerous causes, the most prominent being storms at sea. Energy in the atmosphere is converted through waves at sea into seismic waves in the solid earth. Just how the conversion takes place is complex, but in the 1950s and early 1960s considerable research was done on this subject and a clever mechanism to explain how *part* of the energy is converted was devised. Excellent syntheses were written and the subject, which once occupied many seismologists, now receives little attention. Although it was probably not the intent of the author, the terminal paper(s) left the superficial impression that all was under control in that subject. Attention went elsewhere.

But all is not under control. Only a part of the problem of energy conversion is solved. And the manner in which energy is propagated in the earth from the point of generation of seismic waves to the seismograph station remains poorly understood.

Detailed forecasting of noise at a particular seismograph station, given certain meteorological conditions, is not possible. That fact alone says that there is more to be known. There is, in fact, a great deal more that could be learned about this subject, which is full of nonquestions (see Chapter 2). With the help of a fresh idea, or a new technique, one could surely make discoveries in this neglected subject area and overcome the effect of the "terminal" paper.

Note once again that the terminal paper, as the term is used here, does not refer to a paper that misleads the scientists of a discipline because it is in error. The terminal paper may be fully correct and is not to be faulted. The difficulty and the accompanying opportunity arise because of the erroneous or casual psychological response of the scientific community, which subconsciously and incorrectly interprets the terminal paper as closing the subject.

How does one distinguish between the terminal paper, which seems to mark the end of a subject but does not, and a flattening of the curve of discovery that may indeed indicate that a subject is exhausted of discovery as described in the previous section? The answer is in the observations. If many observations remain unexplained, the field is probably fertile, regardless of the status of scientific papers in that field. If the observations are largely explained or satisfactorily organized, the field is either exhausted or in need of a major program to collect new observations.

F O U R

Personal Traits and Attitudes for Discoverers

T HE "personal traits and attitudes" of this chapter are a selected set of items that seem especially relevant for those bound for discovery. They are not a complete set. For example, some well-known characteristics of those who succeed in science and in other endeavors, characteristics such as drive, perseverance, and fortitude, do not stand out as specific guidelines, although some of those traits appear by inference in other guidelines.

The list of guidelines in this chapter could be much longer. Probably many readers will think of appropriate additions. In any case, the following will provide some provocation.

Never Confuse Sophistication with Understanding

SOPHISTICATION abounds in science. Examples are ubiquitous. A complex device for observation employs esoteric principles and intricate hardware and software. A mathematical technique is tortuous and obscure. A scientific paper is so burdened with intricate jargon that it defies comprehension. It is easy for a young scientist to be caught up in this web of complexity and sophistication and see the perpetuating of it as the sole challenge of science, indeed as the science itself. Sophistication is, however, secondary. It is mostly a means to an end. The basic content and flow of the science are the essence, and that essence should be the objective of the discoverer. The potential discoverer should take care that the search for the basics remains the primary goal and the controlling factor in all decisions.

The great discoveries of science are, once understood, normally rather simple matters, devoid of sophistication and easy to describe or convey. For example, Wegener's basic yet vitally important ideas on the drift of the continents are readily understood. Furthermore, those important concepts can be understood by someone with no knowledge of the esoterics of stratigraphy or petrology, no background in the mathematical theory of deformation of a solid, and no familiarity with precise measurements of rheologic properties of rocks in the laboratory, even though all of these subjects are part of the story. Gaining complete mastery of the subject may call for a learned background, but understanding of the basic concept does not.

Likewise, Wilson's important contribution to plate tectonics, the concept of the transform fault, is easy to understand. Wilson himself lectured on this subject to audiences that often included nonscientists. He conveyed the concept through use of a simple cardboard model. Vine's model, which describes how sea floor spreading at the ocean ridges accounts for the magnetic anomalies of the sea floor, is readily explainable to almost anyone. It may be illustrated by a simple drawing or by analogy with a common tape recorder. Morgan's description of the mobile rigid plates that make up the earth's surface is highly quantitative. It describes the velocity vector of any point on the entire earth's surface relative to any other point. Yet that description is based on Euler's theorem for caps on a sphere, a concept that is taught in early mathematics courses and that, once understood, is a straightforward matter. These ideas are clever and ingenious, but they are not complex and sophisticated in essence.

Sophistication pursued for its own sake is a distraction and a waste. Sophistication is appropriate in science as a means to an end but only if the end is to enhance the fundamental knowledge of the science. Discoveries are made not solely because of sophistication, or solely in spite of it, but because the investigator focuses attention on the elements of the science and is not diverted by the lure of sophistication even though possibly aided by it.

This guideline should not be construed to mean that sophistication is to be avoided in science. Earth science, for example, could not possibly fulfill its potential without using the complexities and power of seismic signal processing, or the elegant software and hardware of image processing, or the application of synchrotron radiation to study materials, or the power of inverse theory, or the unique capability of a deep submersible, or an electron probe, or a spacecraft to another planet. All of the foregoing are sophisticated devices or procedures.

Nor are those scientists who choose to devote their careers to the development of such devices and techniques to be made light of. Far from it. They are essential cogs in the scientific machine. Nevertheless, it must be recognized that such functions, though important, are a peripheral part of the total scientific enterprise and not the mainstream that sets the direction for the science. The lead for direction should fall to those who strive for the main goal, i.e., the enhancement of basic understanding of the object of study, the earth in most examples cited here.

It is important for the potential discoverer to become adept at identifying fundamental science, as distinct from peripheral matters. It is not always easy to do, but the skill must be developed. Practice regularly at scientific meetings. A paper presented orally may be laced with flowery jargon and artistic slides yet be devoid of real advance in the science. It may charm or entrance the beginner or the follower. But such a bedazzled reaction will not come from the seasoned top scientists. If they discuss the paper informally after the meeting, they are likely to do so with a two- or three-sentence summary. The frills will be stripped away and ignored, and only the essence of the paper will be noted and remembered. The ability to go to the heart of the matter and to recognize the essence of a scientific communication is a key characteristic of discoverers.

Enjoy the Struggle, Not the Spoils

A career in science can be difficult, challenging, and rewarding. Science often requires intense concentration, self-sacrifice, unusual perseverance, and long hours of hard work. It demands a high level of personal performance. Consequently, scientists tend to be people who are taken by the challenge of tough going and difficult problems. The best scientists like to overcome obstacles and are willing to work incredibly hard to do so.

Scientists, in other words, thrive on the struggle. They savor the challenge and the fight to conquer it. And they revel in the feeling of success and satisfaction when the challenge is overcome.

Most scientists are not, however, greatly drawn to the spoils of success. They are not given to luxurious and ostentatious styles of living. They are not leaders, or even members, of the jet set. They rarely enjoy leisure for a lengthy period. Of course, I do not mean to say that most scientists do not relish an occasional bottle of fine wine, or a good car, or a pleasant party. They do. But most scientists do not seek a high style of living in return for their efforts and, with few exceptions, most find more enjoyment in the challenge and struggle of the workplace than in the ambiance of a luxurious life-style.

Total dedication is a common characteristic of the discoverer/explorer. I have known scientists who have labored in disease-ridden, steaming tropical jungles; who have ridden small ships in the teeth of the most tempestuous storms at sea; and who have wintered over alone in the Arctic wilds so as to be ready for the spring field season. Such humans are driven by the search for adventure and by the challenge of the scientific problem, but not by hedonism or the thought of material rewards or success.

My indoctrination into geophysical fieldwork took place under the leadership of an especially dedicated and determined scientist named Albert Crary. Crary worked in the Arctic and later became chief scientist for the United States in the Antarctic. He had exceptional drive and perseverance. When he set out to observe something about the earth, he would doggedly pursue that goal in spite of all obstacles and without regard to physical comfort or discomfort.

For example, as we traveled to and through the Arctic, we were sometimes housed at military bases. The military had no uniform policy for accommodating civilian scientists. At some bases we were put up in the elegant quarters normally reserved for generals. At others we were housed in the dingiest of abandoned barracks. Crary took little notice of the difference.

He would not allow the comforts of civilization to distract him or the vagaries of civilization to deter him. When we were to be based for a time at a tiny military outpost on the North Slope of Alaska, Crary made a request of a military officer high in the bureaucracy for 400 square feet of storage and working space for our instruments. The officer granted the request on the spot but added an incredible qualifier when he said firmly "It'll be outside, of course." Now the North Slope is a very large remote, forlorn, inhospitable, and sparsely populated area. It is plagued by cold and wind and drifting snow. To think that Crary was asking for 400 square feet of outside space was preposterous. I was aghast and outraged and wanted to start some drastic action but fortunately deferred to Crary. He knew what to do. He pocketed the written authorization and thanked the officer. Then he walked a few doors down the hall, found another likely officer, repeated the request, without mentioning the earlier attempt, and this time got the authorization he wanted. As we left the building he calmly deposited the first authorization in a trash can. Such adept maneuvering was part of the struggle he enjoyed (see also Chapter 2).

If the plane that transported us to locations on the Arctic pack ice was disabled, or grounded by weather, Crary led us as we set out on foot, dragging our equipment over the rough ice in sleds to work at locations near shore. We built our facilities, operated our instruments, and developed our photographic records under frigid conditions. At lunchtime we thawed our sandwiches one end at a time over a Sterno flame. Crary seemed oblivious to the lack of comfort. He was content under the most inhospitable conditions, so long as the science was going well. And he radiated an enthusiasm for the work and a contempt for self-pity that kept the other members of the party happy under such conditions as well.

The rewards for such deprivation came at those special moments when the observations produced a new idea or a new level of understanding of science. Then, even in the most depressing conditions, the moment of joy appeared. Crary's eyes would light up, his lips and moustache would smile, and satisfaction prevailed—but only briefly until he moved to the next challenge.

Not all scientists operate under such inhospitable conditions as those that Crary thrived upon. But most outstanding scientists have comparable dedication to their work and are more than willing to forego comfort or pleasure to achieve discovery. And the discovery is often as much a stimulus to new effort as a triumph to be reveled in.

Never Fully Accept Any Hypothesis, Theory, Law, or Doctrine

SCIENCE is an unusual kind of endeavor. Those who participate in it and seek to add to it must put intensive effort into it for years, or for life. Yet they can never allow themselves to believe that what they have achieved is fully correct.

Science progresses because of testing of the structure of science against observation, which is the ultimate truth of science. If some part of the structure of science fails to agree with observation, then that structure must be discarded or revised. And it is not merely the recent or proposed additions to science that must be tested. At any time, any and all parts of science, established or not, must be considered as possibly in error and subject to test and revision.

A discovery-minded scientist must have a strange lack of confidence in science and be willing to challenge established parts of science if new observations so demand. He or she must always be open to significant change in the subject and must modify conventional thinking as the need for change is demonstrated.

The discoverer must hold open the possibility that any part of science may be overturned. Science, as Popper has put it, does not prove things correct, but it does prove that some things are incorrect. Nothing in science can ever be proved to be fully correct. Failure to recognize this fundamental nature of science can be a handicap to the discoverer.

Science, in fact, *is* never fully correct. It may be sufficiently correct for almost all practical purposes. It may be so nearly correct that substantial effort in observation is required to improve the approximation. Our understanding of the simple forms of matter is now so good, for example, that huge and elaborate multibillion-dollar devices such as the superconducting supercollider are required just to create the conditions and obtain the observations that will enable us to go beyond our present levels of understanding in this field.

The possibility of modification of science to fit new observations must always be held open. Major revisions of large parts of science occur often. Unfortunately, our teaching of science to beginning students often obscures this point. To such students it may seem that most parts of science are immutable. Of course, there are some parts of science that we feel are less likely to be modified or overturned than others. We try to categorize science on this basis. A law, for example, is a concept so well established that there seems little chance of significant change. That is because the concept seems to fit large and diverse quantities of observations. At the other extreme, a hypothesis may be almost untested by comparison with data. We feel far less certain about its fate. A simple single observation may invalidate a hypothesis. A theory lies somewhere in between a law and a hypothesis with regard to the assurance we attach to its correctness.

We have helped ourselves with this categorization of scientific concepts because we need some crude measure of reliance. The categorization is useful. But we do not want to give the impression, as a staunch term like *law* sometimes does, that some part of science might not someday be overturned or modified.

The researcher must always have the attitude that any law, theory, or hypothesis might be overturned by new observation. And to some, the more established the concept, the greater the challenge of overturning it. That is the spirit that maintains the health of science.

Respect, Not Reverence

THE advanced state of modern science is a consequence of the magnificent efforts of intellectual giants of the past. Contributions of scientists of earlier generations constitute the basis of our science, and those accomplishments serve as an inspiration to all who come later. As a result of their achievements, our predecessors in science deserve the utmost respect of all succeeding generations of scientists. They are entitled to admiration, credit, and honor.

They do not, however, merit reverence. Their work must be challenged, revised, improved, and sometimes discarded. Great as those early efforts may be, they cannot be considered inviolable. As science advances and as observations proliferate, the state of a science changes. What may have been superb performances or exceptional ideas in the past may pale against what can be accomplished in the present or the future.

The modern scientist, therefore, with all due respect for predecessors, must look upon their contributions with an eye to both merit and deficiency. If possible, we build on the foundation they have laid for the future. But if new observations reveal flaws in that foundation, then we must start afresh.

Young people entering science should have no awe of the giants of the past. Their contributions may be well done. But, like all science, their work hangs on available observations. And observations tend to increase in quantity and quality with time. Previous contributions must be continually evaluated and reevaluated in light of new observations. In turn, modern scientists must anticipate a similar reevaluation of their contributions by scientists of the future. Records, as the saying goes in sports, were made to be broken. That spirit also applies in science.

Scientists of the past have often reasoned their way to advances along what we now consider the "right track," only to go astray on some point as a consequence of paucity of observations. For example, Reginald Daly, a professor at Harvard, wrote several books in the 1920s, 1930s and 1940s on various aspects of deformation of the earth. Daly's thinking paralleled that of today in that he emphasized the concept of a strong layer over a weak layer, i.e., lithosphere over asthenosphere, as proposed earlier by others, and the importance of that concept to the understanding of observed earth deformation. Daly thought of the strong layer moving over the weak layer so as to produce deformation in surface rocks, and he postulated a density instability that would cause large pieces of the strong layer to sometimes founder and deform the earth in the process. At a time when many geologists ignored or ridiculed the ideas of Taylor and Wegener concerning continental drift, Daly gave serious consideration and considerable sympathy to those concepts. Daly reasoned his way to an earth model that included some concepts still highly regarded today. But like others unconstrained by observations that would be made later, he also made some errors. He thought, for example, that the asthenosphere, or soft layer, was made of rocks in the vitreous, or glassy, state. That idea is considered incorrect today and, as that idea was disposed of, some of Daly's other ideas for no good reason lost support. And, since Daly's work focused largely on the continents, certain parts of his story were eclipsed when comprehensive observations of the sea floor became available.

During the late 1930s, David Griggs, a Harvard graduate student probably influenced partly by Daly, carried out some interesting model experiments on mountain building. He assumed that subcrustal currents in the mantle were the driving factor in this process. Griggs's work received considerable attention but apparently was not immediately pursued further as World War II intervened, Griggs moved elsewhere, and Daly eventually retired. Nevertheless, Griggs's work would be revived and often cited as the story of plate tectonics was revealed. Thus Daly's influence survived, although some of his immediate contributions did not.

A true giant of the past was Arthur Holmes, a British geologist who, among other things, was instrumental in putting the relative geologic time scale on a firm basis of absolute ages as determined from radioactivity. Holmes's interests in earth science ranged broadly, however. He had a remarkable intuitive sense for how the earth works. His book *Principles of Physical Geology*, originally published in 1944, and later in 1965 in revised version, is still worthwhile reading for any earth scientist. Holmes was an advocate of convection in the mantle as a driving force of surface deformation and was hot on the trail of the relation between subsurface convection and the great geological features of the surface. Griggs's experiments influenced him, but so did a wide variety of other work. He seemed to have a knack for selecting and emphasizing what would later be recognized as truly important. As it was, his contributions to geology were magnificent. But his productive period ended just as the concept of plate tectonics was taking hold. If he had lived a little longer, he would surely have done still more. We cannot fail to respect the work of scientists like Holmes and Daly but we must move on to refine and revise their views as new ideas arise and new data become available.

Let's Hear It for Enthusiasm

I cannot recall ever knowing or hearing of a discoverer who was not enthusiastic. Such enthusiasm is not merely a consequence of successful discovery. Those discoverers were also enthusiastic about their work before discovery. Zest and enthusiasm are important parts of science. Science is not the place for doom-and-gloom, wet-blanket pessimists. It is a place for the optimist, for those who can see light at the end of the darkest tunnel. Sometimes during scientific training so much emphasis is placed on critical review and criticism that it seems that pessimism is a required property of a scientist. The best form, one might think, is to be a "scowl and scoffer."

But experience shows that discovery-minded scientists are far more likely to be eternal optimists. Copy them. If you want to discover, be optimistic. Think positively. Be constructive. Science is a game in which we are trying to move ahead, not drag everything down. Cold, objective testing of every hypothesis is, of course, required in science. But unbridled enthusiasm for the future and what can be accomplished is vital.

There may never have been a more enthusiastic earth scientist than Walter Bucher. Born in the United States and trained in Europe, Bucher spent the bulk of his career as a professor at the University of Cincinnati and at Columbia University. Although his personal research contributions to science were not so monumental as those of some colleagues, Bucher nevertheless enjoyed widespread respect and recognition. He served, for example, as president of both the Geological Society of America and the American Geophysical Union, two of the largest earth science societies.

A centerpiece of his career was his book *The Deformation of the Earth's Crust*. Bucher was eager for progress in geology and no small thinker, and those characteristics were evident in his writing. Furthermore, he was impressed by the rigor and structure of physics and its progress in the early twentieth century. The book is an attempt to bring such rigor to geology and is organized around what Bucher called "Laws," forty-six of them.

The laws were Bucher's effort to generalize various observations of the earth, mostly relating to features of large scale. Accompanying the laws was a set of "opinions," generalizations of less certainty. This rather formal and unusual approach for a descriptive science was an attempt to make the subject more orderly and more manageable. It brought the book, first published in 1933, to the attention of many, including critics. Soon many of the key points of the book were proven, by Bucher's own admission, to be incorrect. A lesser man would have shelved the book and moved onto something less mindful of false steps. But not Bucher. He saw a way to use those errors as a spur to earth science and did not hesitate to do so.

By the late 1940s, when I took his course, Bucher was using the book as a text, pointing out the errors and how he had gone wrong and using the story to stimulate a new generation of earth scientists to attack and solve those great problems he had drawn attention to. He showed time and time again how inadequate observations had led to his demise, and he left his students believing that it was their destiny and their duty to observe the earth thoroughly and so resolve those important matters.

He was on fire with enthusiasm for geology and he lit or fanned that same flame in his colleagues and students, regardless of background. He accepted science students with no prior training in geology into his graduate-level course (it was my first course in geology) in the hope that they would bring information from another field that would be useful in solving problems of the earth. He radiated excitement and bubbled over each time a new piece of information in geology arose. All former students that I know remember him fondly as a professor but even more so as an inspiration. Although he knew little geophysics, he was a stimulus and a key supporter during the formative days of the geophysical program of the Lamont-Doherty Geological Observatory.

At one point during the 1950s, Bucher debated Lester King, the prominent South African geologist, on the subject of continental drift. Bucher was a staunch opponent of drift. In the debate, held in the era preceding the arrival of plate tectonics, Bucher's arguments against drift were noticeably weaker than those he normally presented in class. King won the debate easily and the student body at Columbia was stimulated to discuss continental drift heatedly for many months (unfortunately we then discarded it and had to revive it later). I think Bucher planned it so as to startle us and sacrificed himself in the cause of stimulation of thinking by those students.

The sum total of achievements in geology that bear Bucher's name has likely been surpassed by that of other giants of the field, but if one could somehow tally the collective effects of Bucher's enthusiasm on the work of others, particularly students, his contribution to the science would surely be outstanding. He demonstrated once again that enthusiasm is important and contagious.

There Is No Limit to What You Can Accomplish if Someone Else Gets the Credit

THIS slogan was invented by someone unknown to me and for some other field, but it also applies to science. There is a lot of competition and rivalry in science. The response to one's work by others can be a major factor influencing one's progress. Glory grabbing tends to irk fellow scientists. They may respond by making further progress more difficult. Passing credit freely to whomever and to wherever it is due makes succeeding tasks easier. It is often better to forego an immediate headline for the silent satisfaction of a subsequent major achievement.

It is difficult to provide specific examples of success by someone who has passed the glory on to others, without placing the "others" in a bad light. If readers cannot recall an appropriate example from their own field, surely they can think of many counterexamples in which a leader seeking too much recognition for success lost the support of coworkers and colleagues.

Humility Leads to Discovery

RESEARCHERS working in a given scientific field should, of course, have good knowledge of that field and should use that knowledge in planning their research. That simple statement seems obvious and axiomatic. And in a general way it is. The statement is particularly applicable when the research is in what Kuhn describes as the problem-solving mode, as opposed to the mode of paradigm discovery. There is, however, another side to the coin. It is manifest when the goal is the extraordinary.

Researchers who pride themselves on their knowledge of the subject and who carefully plan their research effort using that knowledge as the sole basis for guidance may do themselves and the science a disservice by limiting their opportunities for discovery. Such scientists may do a very capable job of problem solving or routine science. However, by directing their research narrowly and limiting it to straightforward extrapolation of what they know, they may seriously inhibit unanticipated discovery of a paradigm or extraordinary advance.

Planning research strictly on the basis of what is known today, in other words, limits the range of possible discovery to what can be visualized within the limitations of the knowledge of today. Those limitations may well be so narrow as to exclude the next major discovery. Present knowledge may not lead one to suspect that a particular discovery will occur in the future. In fact, by definition, major discovery will not be fully foreseen. Thus basing research planning solely on present knowledge may be unduly and critically restrictive.

Discovery, in fact, is always accompanied by surprise, usually surprise that something once thought correct is incorrect. In such a situation researchers with the humility to acknowledge that what is known at present may be inadequate, and at least partly wrong, may well design a better research project than researchers will who proceed with the assurance that they know the field well and that existing lore is on a solid basis.

As an example, consider the matter of deep drilling of the continents for scientific, not economic, purposes. Deep drilling is essentially a new tool for basic earth science. Although there has been a great deal of relatively shallow drilling for economic purposes, and extensive drilling of sedimentary basins in the search for petroleum, there has been little deep drilling of the crystalline basement. Deep drilling of the basement has been accomplished at only a handful of places throughout the world. Therefore, the bulk of the continental crust at depth is essentially an unknown frontier so far as sampling and observing by this technique are concerned.

Deep drilling is very expensive. Thus it is obvious that only a limited number of holes will be drilled in the near future. Consequently, the choice of sites for early drilling is critical. A wise or fortunate choice of early sites may result in early major discovery and a strong exploratory program that will continue for decades or centuries. In contrast, failure to make a major discovery early in the program will likely result in less drilling activity in the near future. Even though the potential for discovery will remain, the perception of the worth of a program is highly dependent upon early success. Scientific drilling of the ocean floor during the 1960s provides an example of the latter type. Early in the ocean program it was shown that the ages of crustal rocks as determined from the magnetic anomalies agreed with those measured from fossils obtained by drilling into sediments immediately overlying those same crustal rocks. To some this information, which included demonstration of increasing age with distance from a spreading center, was final confirmation of the hypothesis of plate tectonics and, hence a truly major accomplishment. Oceanic deep drilling has prospered since that early discovery. It has produced many important discoveries although perhaps none so important as its first. The lesson for a continental drilling project is clear. In drilling deeply into the continents, we want to produce a major discovery as quickly as possible in order to gain the early benefit from the discovery and to establish the worth and potential of the technique and thus ensure continuing viability for the program.

The procedure of proposing and selecting a site for deep drilling of the continents reveals two extremes of thinking. On the one hand, some, confident in their knowledge of the earth and the state of the science, propose drilling in an area where a geological problem is well known. Such drilling is designed to provide the answer to that specific problem—and little else. This approach, which in the context of the title of this section brims with confidence and lacks the humility referred to, has the advantage that the task can be impressively spelled out and documented. The approach may, however, represent small thinking so far as major discovery is concerned. Serendipity, in this case, is limited by the boundaries of existing knowledge.

On the other hand, others propose drilling deep into the continent without a special target and solely to explore the unknown. The justification for this approach is that exploration of the unknown nearly always produces major surprises and it is major discovery that we should seek in such a large program. This course is the bolder of the two extremes. It plays on serendipity. It also involves a humility about the extent of mankind's knowledge. Such humility is more compatible with major discovery than the tacit confidence in one's knowledge is, which accompanies drilling into a better-known area with lesser potential.

These two philosophical extremes are cited to make the point of this section. In practice, the basis for selection of a drilling site should prudently include both strategies. A site with a major recognized problem should be drilled at a place where that problem may be solved, but drilling should continue to greater depths and into the unknown in the hopes of making an unanticipated discovery. In fact, the site for the Soviet deep hole in the Kola Peninsula was selected for these dual purposes. This hole is now the deepest in the world. And the more interesting results seem clearly a consequence of the deeper drilling into the unknown. Humility and serendipity strike again!

Audacity Leads to Discovery

AT first glance, it seems somewhat incongruous that humility, the subject of the previous guideline, and audacity, the subject of this one, should both be assets in the quest for discovery. But these two qualities are not exact opposites and each has its place in research.

Humility, in the sense of limited confidence in one's ability to choose the best research problem, need not be accompanied by timidity. Humility does not require that one act cautiously in the choice of a problem. In fact, humility manifested by limited confidence in conventional wisdom may stimulate and trigger the boldness and daring that are important ingredients in a discovery-oriented research effort. Recognition of deficiency in knowledge dictates caution in research activities that involve safety, but it does not dictate lack of boldness in the design of scientific exploration.

As an example, consider the great effort to explore the ocean basins following World War II. That effort was characterized by boldness and daring. But it was predicated on an acknowledged deficiency of information on the ocean basins. The decision to explore the deep sea floor in its entirety was not a consequence of reasoning based on cautious extrapolation of information from land areas into the oceanic areas. It was not, in others words, that the geology of the land areas was used to make a compelling case for studying the oceanic areas. It was rather that the marine areas represented a great unknown, a great frontier that deserved to be explored because it was unknown. There was humility about the basis for the study but audacity in the planning of it.

Boldness counted in this endeavor in other ways. For example, it was audacious to think, as Bullard did, that measuring the temperature gradient over a depth range of only a few meters in the sediments beneath the seas would provide information on heat flow and temperatures deep in the interior. But it does, not in the simple manner that early students of the subject imagined it would, but in more complex but nevertheless revealing fashion.

It was audacious to hope that the earth's gravity field could be measured at sea to a precision of a few parts per million against a background of far larger accelerations (parts per thousand of g) associated with ocean waves. Nevertheless, Vening Meinesz and others, using submarines and elegant instruments with multiple pendulums, did so and found, near the deep sea trenches some of the largest gravity anomalies known and made an observation of major importance.

It was audacious to propose that the entire Antarctic continent could be made accessible to scientific exploration just a few decades after the first humans had reached the South Pole and just after a short history of treacherous and disastrous Antarctic exploration, and yet that continent is now accessible and is far better understood than it was just thirty years ago.

And, of course, it was audacious to send humans to the moon and spacecraft to the planets. Yet it was done.

If one takes a long-term view of history and filters out the short-term difficulties, hurdles, or failures, it seems that humans are destined to achieve what they dare to achieve. The pace of scientific discovery should not be slowed for lack of daring.

Be Optimistic, at Least Secretly

THOSE who make a habit of discovery are optimists. I make that as a flat statement. Perhaps it is true for all those who succeed in any manner. And perhaps somewhere, at some time, somehow, someone who saw only the pessimistic side has happened upon an important discovery in science, but I do not know of any such case.

Now a discoverer is not always optimistic on the surface. Many often appear pessimistic. They worry that a particular experiment will fail, or that a field trip will not be completed for logistical reasons, or that some other impediment to success will arise. Such surficial pessimism may be an asset in that it is an advantage to be alert to impending disaster rather than to be blissfully ignorant of it. Nor does anyone like to be chided for publicly forecasting success when defeat is the outcome.

So some scientists are outwardly pessimistic as a defense against possible failure. If something goes wrong they are then in a position to say "I told you so." But basically, beneath the surface, there is hidden in every discoverer a strong sense of optimism. It is more than a hope that something will go well. It is an inner confidence that it will go well. It is a faith in oneself, in what one is doing, and in science itself. It is not blind confidence that all will always go well, but rather conviction that, in spite of obstacles along the way, at some point all will go well for a time so that the discovery will be made.

Of course, successful people in all walks of life are optimistic and are positive thinkers. Scientists are no different in this regard. Scientists need, however, to avoid the danger that intense training in an objective and very critical manner will mask or subdue the strong sense of optimism necessary to a discoverer.

Avoid All Pretense

PRETENSE has no place in science. Yet it sometimes appears there. Excessive use of jargon in literature or in oral presentations is a form of pretense. False claims with regard to the meaning of an experiment are a form of pretense, unless labeled as speculative. And cleverly and ambiguously worded papers that mislead the reader if interpreted one way and yet are correct if interpreted another are a form of pretense or worse.

Would-be discoverers in science should avoid pretense for two good reasons. One is that it is dishonorable and contrary to the ethics of science to claim or imply something false. The other is that pretense will eventually be revealed, and to the detriment of the pretender. That is the beauty of the scientific method, which continually tests and reevaluates results and conclusions until those parts in error are stripped away and only the correct parts remain. If the parts in error are a consequence of pretense, the pretender will be revealed and recognized by colleagues.

One sometimes hears pretense in a branch of science defended by a scientist of that branch. The justification is that pretense, say, in the form of "scholarly jargon," is needed to maintain the respectability of that branch of science in the eyes of peers in other branches of science. A science should be "professional" they say, in the sense that the information of that science is exclusively for members of that profession. Such reasoning seems foolhardy. Scientists are smart, inquiring people, unlikely to be fooled by any device for long. Once pretense is revealed, the loss is much more detrimental to the pretender than would have been the case with a more straightforward presentation to begin with. Furthermore, any action that inhibits communication of information between branches of science forestalls the possibility of interdisciplinary study or synthesis. Because interdisciplinary areas are uncommonly fertile for discovery, pretense in communication inhibits discovery.

Some scientists are inclined to pretense in dealing with nonscientists, the political sphere, government agencies, or others. Such pretense may be worse than pretense in dealings among scientists, for two reasons. First, there are many smart nonscientists who will see through any pretense. Second, science benefits and prospers when the challenges, the opportunities, and the exciting results of that science are known to the nonscientific world. To obscure or hinder the communication of this information through use of jargon or less than straightforward transmittal of information will surely be detrimental to scientists, as well as nonscientists, in the long run.

A story often told in geophysical circles illustrates in a humorous vein the ultimate in lack of pretense. Two young geophysicists working in the field at a remote location exhausted their funds and so had to wire their supervisor for more money. It was the age of the telegram and the cheapest form of telegram was the night letter, fifty words or less for a very low, fixed price. They chose to use that most economical form of communication. One geophysicist composed the message, politely outlining but not fully describing the desperate situation they were in, finally noting that, if possible, some additional funds would be welcome. But somehow the urgency of their plight was lost in the unruffled language of the first geophysicist, who felt constrained to maintain propriety in the face of an emergency. On reading this tactfully prepared message, the second geophysicist exclaimed, "That's not the way to write a telegram!" He took the pencil and wrote the following, "WE NEED MONEY. WE NEED MONEY. WE NEED MONEY. . . . " and so on for fifty words, the last two, of course, being "WE NEED." The message lacked both tact and pretense. However, the message was clear. The money arrived promptly!

Remember a Scientist's Debt to Society

SCIENTISTS tend to be among the brighter, more gifted, and more talented members of society. Not all are, of course, and there are innumerable bright and gifted people who are not scientists. Nevertheless, scientists fall in a select class, a part of the intellectual elite of the society. And society has recognized that science, and hence scientists, have the potential to contribute significantly to, and hence enhance the level of, the society.

In the present era, scientists are commonly educated, at least at the graduate level and sometimes the undergraduate level as well, at someone else's expense. Once educated, scientists are often supported to do what they choose to do. An individual scientist may be paid to sit in an office and think or write or juggle mathematical symbols. A group of scientists may band together and be supported to probe the nucleus, explore the back of the moon, map the hidden sea floor. What could be nicer? Modern scientists are fortunate. The present is an era of science, the finest era of science in all of earth history. Scientists occupy a privileged position in society as a result.

With a privileged status goes responsibility, however. Scientists are not supported by society because they are nice or talented people. They are supported because they are expected to do something that will eventually return many times over the investment society has made in science.

The something that is returned may take many forms. It might be the basis for a new computer or a new form of energy. Or to use earth science examples, it might be a new way to find petroleum, to understand how and where certain mineral deposits are formed, or to comprehend the vast reservoir of subterranean water and the way that reservoir is perturbed by human activities. Or scientists might provide information valuable in governing, waging war, or maintaining peace.

Or the something that is returned might be less practical and more intellectual. We might satisfy the curiosity of all humans about the nature of the moon, the origin of the great mountain ranges of the earth, or the causes of volcanoes and earthquakes. There are many things that science can and does do for the human race.

Scientists must be continually alert to their responsibility and their need to return value in kind to the society. Science must govern itself so as to ensure that the scientific enterprise is carried out in the most effective, economic, and productive manner. Scientists must discourage expenditure of funds and effort on trivia (no easy task in a world where discovery can spring unexpectedly from an obscure source) and must always be alert to possible application of their results in ways that will benefit society.

Of course, science cannot always produce advances that will fit neatly the time scale of quarterly or annual reports. It may take years or decades before some kinds of science produce rewards. However, science and scientists can, and should, continually reevaluate not only scientific projects but also the internal workings of the scientific community so as to optimize the scientific effort. It is irresponsible for scientists to say, as a few have done, that they refuse to work on anything with a sign of practical application. That is an undeserved slap in the face of the people who foot the bill. Society, on the other hand, must tolerate the wasted or unproductive effort that inevitably results as science explores the unknown. Society has done so in the past and will likely continue to do so, provided it remains convinced that the scientific enterprise is operating effectively. Scientists have run their activities so as to maintain that confidence in the past. We must continue to do so. And we must counter any forces tending to put science in the position of an entitlement or welfare program of the future. It is only fitting that those with the above-average talents that most scientists enjoy give more to the society than they receive.

Dream a Little, or a Lot

THE successful discoverer or innovator is commonly a dreamer who spends substantial intervals of time visualizing what might be done differently and what consequences, usually pleasant ones in the dreams, will result from an imaginative new way of doing something.

This guideline is a recommendation to dream a little, or more if it seems productive. Of course, I am not recommending that, as a young employee, you let your first boss catch you with your feet on the desk, your eyes on the ceiling, and your mind on the Super Bowl game. Nor do I recommend that you show your boss this book if you are so caught! But I do suggest that you do an appropriate amount of dreaming, that you consciously and continually encourage your mind to explore new ways to do things and new ways to understand things.

Dreaming is an important component of creativity of any sort. An innovator continually imagines radically new ways of doing things and probes new combinations of activities that may produce beneficial interactions. The innovator seeks new perspectives on problems and attacks classes of problems that are foreign to the innovator but that might yield to his or her special background or experience.

Although it seems obvious that some exploratory mental adventures, i.e., dreams, must be an important component of discovery thinking, the routine demands of everyday activities may preclude an appropriate amount of "dream time." The investigator may need to improve performance and productivity by consciously scheduling or allocating some time to this important function. Of course, great ideas cannot be scheduled, but the chances of having a great idea can be enhanced by appropriate encouragement of the mind.

For me, regularly scheduled dream time occurs when I am walking to and from work, or during a stroll at lunchtime, and sometimes following the reading of journals received in the afternoon mail. There are other spontaneous intervals as well.

So when you come across some observations that do not fit the standard explanation, let your mind wander to see whether some radically different interpretation might do a better job. Perhaps you will think of something that will fit both the new data and the old data and thereby supplant the standard explanation. Toy with different perspectives. Look for the unusual. Try consciously to innovate. Train yourself to imagine new schemes and innovative ways to fit the pieces together. Seek the joy of discovery.

Always test your new thoughts against the facts, of course, in rigorous, cold-blooded, unemotional scientific manner. But play the great game of the visionary and the innovator as well.

Occasionally, Think Like a Child

ONE of the principal consequences of a modern scientific education is that one learns to reason in a complex way about intricate matters. To do so is an important part of science, and to learn to do so is a necessary part of a scientific education. The process carries with it, however, the danger that the scientist will lose sight of the basic goals and the basic questions of the science because they seem too simple to be a part of the frontiers of science. Some of those questions are so straightforward that they might be asked by an inquisitive child. Discovery-oriented scientists need occasionally to think like a child and ask and reiterate those very basic questions about their science.

What, for example, are some of those questions in the case of earth science? "Why is the earth round?" is something a child might ask. It is a fundamental question and might occur to anyone, trained or untrained, while looking at the globe. The answer to that particular question seems well in hand now that we recognize the effects of gravity and that rocks of the interior yield readily, in contrast to the brittle behavior of those rocks we find at the surface of the earth.

But not all childlike questions about the earth are already answered. How about "Why is the earth's surface part land and part water?" That basic question is not fully answered at present, nor is "Why are the continents shaped like that?" a childlike question that we are just beginning to attack. Or how about "What makes an earthquake?" or "Why are there mountains here and not there?" or "Why is that volcano erupting now?" Such questions might all be asked by children. At best they are only partially answered by modern science. Questions of this nature are often among the most fundamental of the science, and an occasional relisting and review of them, particularly in light of the most recent observations and thinking, may be stimulating for the discovery-minded scientist.

The admonition to think like a child is certainly not new on these pages. Prominent scientists have followed this practice and urged others to do so regularly in the past. Perhaps the most noteworthy example was Albert Einstein. Holton draws attention to a statement by Einstein to the effect that he succeeded in good part because he kept asking himself questions concerning space and time that only children wonder about.

It may be, of course, that many scientists recognize the value of thinking about science in this very simplified fashion, but only a limited few are willing describe it in that manner.

I can recall attending, as a beginning student, a major national scientific meeting at which one of the sessions was devoted to the study of sediments on the ocean floor. Most of the papers were characterized by jargon and esoteric problems that were difficult for the beginner to comprehend. The sediments were described by terms like *calcilutite* and *foraminiferal ooze* that held important meaning for the initiated but that left out the newcomer. One speaker, however, somewhat to the embarrassment of some colleagues and students, referred to the deep ocean sediments by the simple term *mud*. While this term would have been inadequate for reporting most studies, it served his purposes well, for he was attacking one of the most fundamental considerations of that time, the total volume of sediments that has accumulated in the ocean basins throughout their history. It was a simple childlike question in essence. He approached it in the most direct, straightforward, frill-free manner, but the importance to the science was so fundamental that no one could possibly make light of the effort regardless of the simplicity of the approach and the language. Maintaining childlike wonder and fascination and thinking in the absence of constraints imposed by modern science are often assets to the would-be discoverer.

Work Hard, Then Harder

WORKING hard is a secret to success in almost any field, and science is no exception. Not all individuals have the same talents. Some are better endowed naturally then others. But nearly everyone has some substantial talents and assets. And no one, whether more talented or less talented, ever uses all assets to full capacity. Hard work is the means of stimulating more effective use of one's talents. Thus someone who is modestly gifted may surpass someone who is more so, simply by working harder. This observation is an often repeated one. It is as valid in modern society as it has been in the past and is likely to remain so in the future.

Scientists who are caught up in the fascination of discovery often work night and day, day in and day out, weekends and holidays, at least during their peak discovery periods. Sometimes the work is exhausting; sometimes it is drudgery. Nevertheless, it is done and those who do it best and fastest have the inside track to discovery.

Examples of hardworking scientists who have produced discovery are numerous. None needs to be cited here. It is easy for anyone to observe this phenomenon at work at any thriving research institution.

To put the content of this section in other terms, the message of Horatio Alger lives—in science and elsewhere. Hard work, perseverance, honor, and integrity are a major part of the route to success. Call it old-fashioned if you like. It's true. Hard work works.

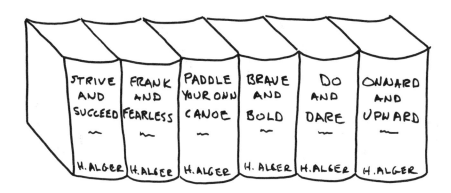

Some Characteristics of an Innovator

LEADERS of large companies have told me that, of all personnel hired specifically to discover, less than 10 percent, perhaps closer to 5 percent, succeed in discovering. This figure demonstrates a well-known point. It is very difficult indeed to select a potential innovator before the actual innovation. It would be advantageous if a better job of selecting potential discoverers could be accomplished before discovery.

To some extent the problem must be unresolvable. Fate is always a factor in discovery. Good fortune is required in addition to the talents and skills of the individual. It must be, however, that some people are better equipped than others to achieve discovery, and criteria to help in their selection would be useful.

The following are some qualities that I think are common to many individuals who have been successful discoverers. The list is certainly not comprehensive, but it may be of some value for those involved in the selection process. No order of priority or importance is intended by order in the list.

1. Radiant enthusiasm
2. Elation on discovery
3. Drive and perseverance
4. A penchant for dreaming
5. Dissatisfaction with the status quo
6. Abhorrence of the familiar
7. The knack of seeing things in different light
8. A strong urge to win
9. Willingness to depart from the norm in dress, cars, and habits
10. Joy on revealing something new to colleagues
11. Appreciation for the beauty of simplicity
12. An urge to add another item to this list

F I V E

Caveats

N o one, least of all a young scientist, likes to hear a lot of warnings or restraints. This chapter on caveats includes, therefore, only three guidelines. The younger readers who have a tendency to mistrust the establishment (of which I am unquestionably a part) will probably like these particular caveats, all of which challenge established views of some sort.

Beware of Indoctrination

For most practitioners of science, the more thorough and nearly complete the background in science, the better. That statement seems obvious. We need the advantage of cumulative experience and knowledge as we use science to best advantage. There may, however, be an important exception to the foregoing generalization. An intensive indoctrination in a particular branch of science may not be the best route to major discovery in that field. Many major discoveries in one branch of science have been made by those trained largely in another branch. It may well be that too thorough an indoctrination in a particular discipline inhibits the scientist's capacity for breaking away from convention in that discipline. A discoverer should not be confined to, or led down, the same lines of reasoning followed earlier by others. Those less initiated into a science may have a more advantageous position for discovery in that science than those heavily indoctrinated in it.

The sword is double-edged, of course. It is risky to plunge into an unfamiliar subject populated by experienced practitioners. One who knows little or nothing about a science may propose hypotheses that are readily contradicted by observational facts and hence that turn out to be nonsense. And the voices of experience will surely point that out. The other side of the coin is, however, that those already familiar with the observations and with the conventional ways of accounting for them may never recognize inadequacies in the conventional approach. A shrewd newcomer may be able to overturn conventional thinking.

Lack of overindoctrination may partially account for the relatively high incidence of important discoveries by young scientists. Young workers sometimes seek and find discovery in areas written off or bypassed by older workers, solely because the young do not know, or accept, that such areas "should" be bypassed.

In earth science, and other sciences as well, not all major discoveries are made by young scientists by any means. In fact, the average age of discovery is likely higher for earth science than for many other sciences because of the highly observational nature of earth science. It takes time to develop a comprehension of the facts. Nevertheless, young scientists do make a disproportionately large contribution. And it seems clear that discovery does not increase regularly with age for all individuals, as it should if indoctrination into the science were the only factor involved.

Perhaps the most dramatic example of discovery in earth science by a relative outsider is Wegener's development of the concept of continental drift. Wegener was trained in astrophysics and practiced meteorology. Nevertheless, he was able to recognize the great opportunity in geology when solid earth scientists did not and was able to capitalize on it regardless of limited indoctrination in the subject. Wegener pursued the subject relentlessly in considerable detail and depth, familiarizing himself with a wide variety of observations and using them in support of the hypothesis. Wegener's success may be the classic case of major discovery by a scientist not indoctrinated in that branch of science.

At the opposite end of the spectrum, so far as earth science is concerned, is the attempt by Lord Kelvin to determine the age of the earth. Kelvin was a brilliant, highly respected, physicist. He had an outstanding record in science. The temperature scale, for example, is named after him. He attempted, however, to move into earth science and experienced major failure. He used the tools of mathematical physics to calculate the age of the earth based on a simple physical model for its cooling. He obtained an age that we now know, and that geologists of that day knew, was much too short. He argued strongly for this age, in spite of geological evidence, with which he was not very familiar, to the contrary. Eventually, the evidence and the geologists prevailed. It was a classic example of error because of too little indoctrination.

These two stories illustrate a characteristic of the unindoctrinated. They are more readily able, and more likely, to go beyond the bounds of convention in a science than the indoctrinated are. Going beyond the bounds may sometimes mean spectacular success. It may mean major discovery not envisioned by the indoctrinated. Or it may also mean ignominious failure. The scientist who enters an unfamiliar branch of science is gambling. But there is an important role in science for those who take the risk of breaking out and who strike out in a favorable direction. Consider breaking into a new field if you have a solid background in basic science. Scrutinize the opportunity carefully and if it is promising, make a move. You may not be welcomed with open arms by the cognoscenti of that field, but you may capitalize upon an opportunity they have overlooked.

Beware of Occam's Razor

THE term "Occam's razor" is used to refer to the principle that the simplest explanation is the best. It is named for William of Occam, a fourteenth-century English philosopher. This principle is so widely taught and widely known in science that it becomes second nature for a scientist to act according to the principle, which is a valuable one in science. It is often, however, misused and is often the cause of misdirection and lost opportunity in science. The simplest explanation is the best. *But* it is only the best when and if *all* observations bearing on the matter at hand are considered.

One should not apply Occam's razor indiscriminately if only subsets of the data relevant to a problem are available. One should not, for example, find models to satisfy each of several subsets of the data that bear on a problem and then hope that all of the subset models will fit together into a grand model that will explain the complete set of data. Such thinking has often led us astray and into confusion.

As an example consider the large negative gravity anomalies associated with the oceanic trenches of the island arcs. These anomalies are prominent and are an important piece of information relating to global tectonics. They are, however, only a subset of the total set of data bearing on the arcs or on global tectonics.

From the time the anomalies were first discovered, geophysical models were proposed to account for them. One early suggestion was that they were a consequence of plastic deformation that resulted from compression normal to the arc. It was postulated that there was a symmetric downbuckling of lighter surface materials into the more dense materials below and, hence, a deficiency of mass that produced the anomaly. Another early, but completely different, explanation was that the trenches were a consequence of extension. In this model the crust was thinned and the rock surface depressed beneath the trenches. The "missing" rock accounted for the anomaly. Other explanations were proposed as well, but these two sharply contrasting examples illustrate the wide differences in the tectonic history implied by the different models. Contraction was the essence of one model, extension the essence of the other. Yet these two models and all the intermediate ones fit the limited gravity data. Each seemed to its originator an explanation of minimum complexity, in the style of Occam's razor.

With the discovery of plate tectonics, it became evident that near-rigid plates of lithosphere were descending into the interior at a modest angle of dip beneath the arcs. The process is a key element of plate tectonics and it is termed *subduction*. The gravity anomaly was accounted for by the mass distribution that resulted from the subduction process and related phenomena.

Now plate tectonics may be the simplest model that fits the observational data of all types for the entire earth and hence is an "Occam's razor" solution on that scale. But what plate tectonics demands for the structure of the island arc, and it is a structure that also fits the gravity data, is by no means as simple as models that were envisioned to explain, and did explain, the gravity data alone. Occam's razor was improperly applied in the early studies based solely on gravity data, because only a subset of the total data set bearing on global tectonics was used.

Or, put in another way, if someone beginning with the gravity data, and gravity data alone, had, through some inspiration, correctly proposed the plate tectonics model, he or she would have had to violate the principle of Occam's razor to do so.

This one example does not do justice to the widespread and pernicious effects of misapplication of Occam's razor. It operates at all levels of activity in science, from glorious global theory to ordinary day-to-day concerns. Consider an example of the latter.

Some years ago my attention was drawn to evidence for post-glacial faulting in the northeastern United States and adjoining parts of Canada. The typical evidence for such faulting is found at a road cut where the glacially polished surface at the top of the road cut outcrop shows striations offset, typically, on the order of a centimeter. It is a small effect but a distinct one. Because the striations are offset, the date of faulting must be poststriation (or postglacial). Thus the faulting must have occurred within about the last ten thousand years. The typical reaction by some geologists to such evidence at a single outcrop is conditioned by Occam's razor. They leap to the simplest explanation, which is that either the outcrop has slumped a bit following construction of the road cut or, if there is evidence of blasting, that explosives shifted the rock during construction. Both are reasonable explanations given those limited data, but both are wrong. After looking at many such road cuts, and many other outcrops away from road cuts and with similar evidence for faulting, the geologist recognizes that the simplest solution based on limited data is wrong. In fact, the pattern is consistent over much of the region and so must involve a regional, as opposed to a local, phenomenon. The geologist was betrayed, or was undercut (!) by subconscious reliance on Occam's razor.

Misuse of Occam's razor does not always follow the pattern

decribed above, i.e., focus on observations of a feature of small scale while ignoring data on those of larger scale. The difficulty does not arise simply because of differences in scale. It arises because of consideration of only a limited fraction of the relevant data.

For example, the once widely held hypothesis that deformation of the earth's surface was largely a consequence of contraction due to cooling of the entire earth certainly involved features of large scale. And the model was a simple one in Occam's razor style. But the model failed because it explained only a subset of the observational data that related to the compressional mountain ranges, all located on land. Once a greater data set was considered, one that included the extensional features, particularly the midocean rift system, as well as the compressional ones, the contraction model, simple and beautiful as it was, had to be discarded.

Occam's razor is an important tool in science, but it is also a potential pitfall. Those who do not use it carefully and appropriately may mislead themselves and the science. A discoverer can turn this phenomenon to advantage by recognizing it and by searching for past misuse of Occam's razor. Discovery may be waiting for those who rectify such misuse.

Beware of Classification Schemes

IN searching for an opening in science that might produce discovery, here is one way to start. Reconsider classification schemes.
In other words, return to the basics, the observations that are
the foundation of science. Then ask whether classification
schemes devised in earlier eras are optimum in the modern world
of science. The retrospective view is a great advantage. Use it. Do
not be lulled into a sense of security and finality as a consequence of the overindoctrination in the present organization of
science that your education has given you.

Of course, classification schemes are beneficial. They must be
devised and used. They are demanded by the need to organize
the huge and otherwise overwhelming volume of observations in
science. We must strive to develop a simple framework for order-
ing of observations and discussion of those observations. Classification schemes are useful tools and a basis for progress in
science.

But any particular classification scheme can be hazardous,
misleading, and intellectually confining as well. It can be a trap
that limits our thinking to certain prescribed channels and inhibits our efforts to see our basic data in a fresh light.

The quality, utility, and versatility of a classification scheme
all vary greatly from one scheme to another. Some seem a consequence of exceptional inspiration. They endure indefinitely. They
readily accept new and unanticipated observations that seem to
fall unambiguously and naturally within the bounds set by the
classification scheme. Other such schemes are less versatile. They
may be adequate for the limited data on which they were based.
However, new and unanticipated data may fail to fit smoothly
into the classification scheme. Attempting to force new observations into a scheme that they do not fit inhibits discovery. Instead, the scheme should be abandoned.

Often, observations are forced into a classification system in
spite of ambiguity. For those who are completely familiar with
both the data and the scheme, the obfuscation may be minor.
They can maintain in their heads a sense of discrepancy and its
importance. However, those who come later may not be made
aware of the inconsistencies. If they are indoctrinated with the
classification scheme under the implicit assumption that it ade-

quately describes the data they may be sadly misled, and an opportunity for discovery may be missed.

As an example, consider the crust-mantle boundary discussed in a previous section. The crust-mantle boundary for many years was, and still is by most scientists, equated with the Moho, a seismologically observed boundary at which the seismic velocity increases from about 7 km/sec to about 8 km/sec. The seismological change is typically abrupt so the boundary is sharp and distinct. Thus all rocks just below the Moho are classed as part of the mantle and all rocks above as part of the crust. So long as the typical situation prevails, no difficulty arises. But all is not typical and difficulty does arise. Sometimes, for example, the boundary is sharp but the velocity of the subboundary rocks is 7.6 km/sec, not 8 km/sec. It's just "anomalous mantle," someone says, striving to preserve the classification scheme that has been taught as correct. But wait, at some places the rocks above the discontinuity have a velocity of 7.4 km/sec. That should be part of the crust, according to the scheme. But the measuring technique is such that the difference between 7.4 and 7.6 km/sec may be insignificant. In other words, in some cases there may be little or no observational basis for distinguishing rocks of the crust in one place from rocks of the mantle in another. Such an observation may well be an important and critical fact about the earth, but it may go unrecognized indefinitely because the scientific community is heavily indoctrinated in a classification scheme (crust and mantle) that tends to force the distinction and bury or obscure observations that do not fit neatly into the scheme.

The discovery-bound scientist who investigates classification schemes will find many opportunities. Even the simplest of schemes have flaws. Are all rocks sedimentary, igneous, or metamorphic? Well, hardly. There are sediments of volcanic origin, migmatites, (part igneous and part metamorphic), and metasediments all falling between the simple categories. It is probably correct to say that all classification schemes are imperfect. And in that zone of imperfection often lies information that has not been so carefully examined for discovery as the information has that falls in the mainstream of the current classification scheme. The grass is not always greener on the other side of the fence, but it is often longer and greener beneath the fence.

SIX

A Few Views and Comments on Science

T HE subjects for the views and comments of this chapter are selected ones, selected because they may influence the scientist's choice of a path to discovery. Some are philosophical. Some scientists bypass the philosophy of science, holding it in abeyance while they get on with their work of advancing science. But to do so is sometimes to join the crowd that is rushing blindly ahead in the name of science without appreciating what course is being followed. Often the strategy for a major scientific project depends upon the philosophical perspective of science held by the leader of the project, and that strategy is the key to discovery.

Other topics deal with the way science is organized or the way it operates. Such topics are fertile ground for the discoverer. Find a weak spot or gap in the current structure and you may find a major discovery waiting. Some topics are related to the ability to recognize quickly an important discovery made by yourself or another. Other topics may also put the scientist in a position of enhanced opportunity for discovery. Many of the topics are fair game for criticism by those with different perspectives, but all of them deserve consideration by the would-be discoverer.

How, Not Why

QUESTIONS in science often begin with the word "why." The implication is that the scientist will, indeed, know or find out "why" a particular phenomenon happens as it does. That is unfortunate, for strictly speaking we scientists never discover "why" anything happens. At best, we discover "how" something happens. Modern science is basically empirical. We collect observations. Then we find ways, often very clever ways, to organize those observations. We try to bring any and all observations, no matter how diverse, within one single organizational structure. The structure is thus a complex one made of laws, theories, concepts, hypotheses, etc. It is an elegant and beautiful structure built with great effort, exceptional ingenuity, and powerful reasoning by brilliant humans. But the structure is good only when it fits the observations, bad when it does not. Although some would like to believe that as we build our scientific structure we are revealing fundamental truths at a philosophical level not previously penetrated, it is by no means obvious that we are. It is only obvious that we are having some success in organizing observations in a manner that allows us to comprehend those observations, and hence the physical world, more readily.

Some may challenge this simple description of science on the grounds that it ignores or bypasses the so-called scientific method in which a hypothesis is proposed and then tested by experiment. However, I see this part of science as merely procedural and not the essence of science. Experiments are only a means of obtaining a particular kind of observation, and the proposing of a hypothesis is merely a step in the organization of observations. Nor is this particular procedure, i.e., the scientific method as described here, the only valid means of advancing science. Exploration of the unknown in the absence of a hypothesis is a perfectly valid way to proceed in science and often a preferable one if major discovery is the goal.

Some see something more powerful or meaningful in the ability of science to predict what will happen. By "predict" they imply that observations of the future will follow the same pattern as observations of the past that have already been organized by science. This view capitalizes on the mystique that accompanies the unknown, in this case the future. In terms of the ultimate meaning of science, however, and with the possibility of change in the laws of science with time omitted, there seems no significant difference between the ability to forecast observations of the future and the ability to describe past observations not known when the relevant part of science was formulated. The prediction capability is, in my opinion, overinterpreted. In short, modern science, wonderful as it is, is empirical. It answers the question of how something happens and never why something happens.

Although some scientists, some philosophers, and numerous nonscientists anticipate that science will someday answer the great questions of philosophy or reveal the fundamental motivation for nature, in fact there is no sign of progress in this direction. The how we do; the why seems out of reach.

Keeping constantly aware of science's capability for the how, and science's limitation for the why, may influence one's course in science, and hence affect the process of personal discovery. The emphasis in science should be on the observations and the organization of those observations. The alternative, emphasis on the involved, complex, and often misleading theoretical structure of science, is, in the absence of strong grounding in the observations, more likely to lead one astray. That is not to say that expenditure of effort on theory in science is misplaced or unnecessary. Far from it. We need adventuresome theoreticians as much as we need adventuresome explorers. But we must keep in mind that the ultimate truth in science is observation.

Recognition of the fundamental "how, not why" limitation of science has implications far beyond the purview of this book on discovery. Many modern persons, it seems, have abandoned philosophical or religious approaches to the answers of the great questions of life, apparently, and perhaps subconsciously, because of an implicit faith that science will someday answer those questions. I am a strong and enthusiastic supporter of science but cannot see any sign that science has that capacity or that potential. Science is empirical, not mystical or spiritual. We mislead ourselves if we think otherwise.

A Science Among the Sciences

WE live in a remarkable time that future historians will likely designate the era of science. Never before has there been such rapid expansion of scientific knowledge as in the last few centuries. Never before have humans understood nature to the levels of the present. Never before has there been such widespread appreciation of science, so much support for science, so many humans engaged in science as at present. And the pace is accelerating. This is a time like no other in history. Modern practitioners of science are fortunate to have been born for this era. Nonscientists are fortunate to benefit from science-based technological advances that currently appear at unprecedented rates.

In the face of this great boom in science, we must ask ourselves where science is going. What does the future hold? Now that the worth of science is demonstrated and rather widely accepted, will science continue to prosper and grow indefinitely, or will it, like other human ventures, falter and diminish at some future time?

The answer to such a question is not simple, for many factors may affect the future of science. To some extent the health and longevity of science is a societal and political matter dependent upon the decisions of the society regarding emphasis and support. The role of such matters will surely be important, but that aspect of the future of science is not discussed in detail here, except to note the obvious point that such support will probably continue only so long as science provides benefits to the society.

There is the more fundamental question, however, of whether science *can* grow indefinitely with opportunity for new discovery always readily available. Are the opportunities for science unlimited? In other words, is the total body of scientific knowledge, both that currently known and that currently unknown and remaining to be discovered, finite or infinite? Or to put it another way, will scientific discoveries some day run out, so that no matter how hard we try, nothing new will be learned?

Posed to a diverse group of scientists, that question would probably evoke a variety of responses. Some would say that the universe is so vast and complex that the opportunity for discovery may be thought of as effectively infinite for the present and the foreseeable future, regardless of whether it is actually so. On the other hand, some would see a time in the distant future when everything of significance and interest that can be known about nature will have been discovered, and hence, opportunities for discovery will be limited to subjects once known and then forgotten. And the answer may well depend upon whether one considers the whole of nature (in a finite or infinite universe) or a well-defined, finite subset of nature, perhaps a particular scientific discipline. The purpose of this discussion is not to resolve the basic question for all science but rather to evaluate it for a particular limited part of science, a somewhat easier task.

Before proceeding further along this theme, let us note that almost all scientists *act* as though the opportunity for important discovery were unlimited, or at least so large as to appear unlimited at present. A major discovery in some field, for example, does not discourage further activity in that field. Often just the opposite happens. Major discovery stimulates more work in the field or specialized parts of it, presumably with the hope that such study will lead to additional major discoveries. And, of course, it may be that, at least in some cases, this view is correct.

However, when a particular, limited subdiscipline of science is considered, it is apparent that such an attitude may be incorrect. At some point, it may be that all the major discoveries of that subdiscipline have been made. If so, it is important for the would-be discoverer to recognize or sense that situation and act accordingly, i.e., move efforts elsewhere. Thus subjective judgment about when a subdiscipline is exhausted of major discovery is an important element of the art of discovery.

Consider an example I have used before, one of the early phases in the history of exploration of the earth, the geographical exploration of the earth's surface. This great human adventure grew slowly over many millennia, then suddenly blossomed just a few hundred years ago. Then during a few lifetimes, a time interval very short compared with the age of the earth or the duration of human existence, all major discoveries about the configuration of the earth's surface were made. Humans learned what the entire surface of the earth looks like, for the first time in history.

It was a magnificent and exciting period of discovery, but it ended more quickly than it began. The subject is now exhausted. There are no more continents to discover, no new island chains to find, no more poles to reach. The time of new discovery in geographical exploration of the earth's surface is over so far as discovery of major features is concerned. A would-be discoverer would be foolish to choose this subject in the hope of finding a major new continent, for example.

Because the geography of the earth's surface is known to us all, it is easy to make and recognize the point in this case. By analogy we can see that opportunity for major discovery in other branches of science may rise and fall in similar fashion. In any finite subject, there is, after all, only a finite number of interesting features to observe and hence observations to be made. Of course, it is always possible to make more and more detailed observations, but at some level, interest wanes. To draw on my earlier example from geography, few would care about the precise location of the grains of sand that define a beach, even though the beach itself and certainly the land of which it is a part were geographical discoveries of some interest. It is the threshold of interest that ensures that the observations of a given subdiscipline of science are finite and manageable.

I can use this example in analogy with other branches of science. The exploration of other parts of the earth, a major fraction of the science of geology, is likely to be finite in the same sense. At some time in the future, scientists will have made all the observations of interest that can be made of the earth. Once these observations are appropriately organized into the best possible self-consistent view of earth and earth history, the time of discovery in geology will be almost over. Of course, there may be geological discoveries to be made on planets, moons, asteroids, etc., and they will affect the organization of observations of the earth somewhat but probably not so seriously as to affect the basic story of earth derived from observations of earth.

The importance of this rather lengthy argument is to make the point that scientific discovery in geology, and probably in most or all branches of science, is finite. Strategy in exploration may be strongly affected by this view. An experimenter striving to learn about a subject may do one thing if the subject appears finite, another if it seems infinite. Such decisions may be an important component of thinking for discovery.

To some extent the effect is psychological. A scientist who sees an endless frontier ahead may be satisfied with only a modest advance that can be fit into the evolving existing structure. An ambitious scientist who sees the opportunity for discovery as finite is more apt to plan a forward-looking, all-encompassing effort that will have the potential to complete major discovery in the entire subject. It is upon such relatively subtle differences in attitude that the art of discovery rests.

Will Science Stifle Itself

WHETHER science is stifling itself is of immediate importance to the discoverer. If science is being held back by things scientists have conditioned themselves to do, individually or collectively, then one needs only to find ways to break through those barriers to open a road to discovery.

Consider one trend in science in the post–World War II years. Many forces within the structure of science act so as to drive the scientist toward greater and greater specialization. A young scientist must specialize in order to progress in science. Theses and scientific papers are more readily accepted by journals and by the scientific community if highly specialized. Organizations hiring scientists tend to choose employees according to skill in the particular specialty that is in demand at that time. University departments, for example, typically seek a specialist in a particular field that will "round out" the department.

Funding agencies, often swamped by increasing numbers of proposals and proposers, divide their organization into programs corresponding to narrower and narrower specialties. Program directors and reviewers tend to discredit or downgrade proposals that extend beyond the specialty and that would hence divert funds from the specialty to other areas. One of their goals is to maximize funds for the specialty, not for science as a whole or for the good of society as a whole.

Jargon is a major factor in the confinement of scientists to specialties; the more jargon, the more difficult it is to move into new areas. Publishers encourage specialization by initiating a journal in a specialty as soon as that specialty becomes sufficiently well recognized and well staffed so that libraries are forced to subscribe. Directories list innumerable specialties; awards are given for accomplishments in a specialty; advanced classes are all in one specialty or another.

The drive toward specialization is not all bad. Much of it is good. Science is far too complex and too broad for a beginning scientist to accomplish much without focusing on a very narrow topic. It is only through specialization that most topics can be probed to great depth. A widespread array of specialists ensures that someone will know something about each recognized topic of science, even though none will know about everything and few about many things. In this sense, specialization is indeed a blessing, providing collective understanding far beyond that of the ancient natural philosopher who tried to know something about everything or everything about everything.

But there is danger in specialization as well. As specialization grows, science tends to become fragmented. Specialists talk only to others in that specialty. Few attempt to cross the barriers between specialties and to synthesize data from many specialties in ways that would lead to broader understanding. Few develop the multidisciplinary hypotheses that can, in turn, stimulate the specialties.

Sometimes specialists focus on problems so narrow as to be completely removed from reality. In such cases, a supposed branch of science may be but a fiction in the brains of the specialists and of limited value in understanding the real world or in interaction with other sciences. Or science can become professionalized as science only for scientists, or as a specialty only for specialists, just as, for example, law sometimes seems only for lawyers, medicine only for physicians, engineering only for engineers, and Little League baseball only for parents.

The overpowering drift toward specialization is not irreversible. Overspecialization may be characteristic of the period described by Kuhn as the time of normal science or puzzle-solving science. When such periods are interrupted by the development of a new paradigm, it affects and alters the entire structure of science, including the specialties. It forces specialists to see their branch of science in light of the paradigm and hence in light of other specialties. In a short time barriers are broken and specialties are intermixed. Inexorably, division of the science into new specialties begins.

In retrospect, it is obvious that earth science experienced such a breaking down of old specialties and formation of new specialties during the plate tectonics revolution. The great global synthesis based on the moving plate model forced all specialists to broaden. Almost overnight, for example, specialized journals that once seemed of little interest and almost unintelligible to a specialist of a different field suddenly became readable and fascinating to all. The curse of specialization that had narrowed our interest and our lives had been broken and new views of science were enjoyed by all.

Now that plate tectonics is well established and the ferment over its introduction has died away, earth science seems to be reverting gradually to its earlier state. Specialties are flourishing and specialists proliferating.

The would-be discoverer who maintains a detached view may find opportunity by consciously recognizing the boundaries of the specialties and particularly the gaps between specialties. As in the case of classification schemes (see Chapter 5) the transgression of the boundaries and the occupying of the gaps between specialties may be the keys to important discovery. In the process the discoverer can also counteract to some degree the stifling of science by itself.

Science has also begun to stifle itself as a consequence of its own success. It has developed a cadre of researchers in such numbers, and opportunity in research in such variety, that capability and opportunity regularly outstrip support. The numbers of good research scientists have grown in almost every field. No longer are there but a few individuals at a small number of select universities capable of leadership in the science. Now almost all major universities have highly qualified scientists in a wide variety of fields. All are skilled in research and fully capable of running research projects. The demand for funding has gone up accordingly.

Furthermore, scientists, in general, have raised their hopes, their aspirations, and their appetites. It is no longer unusual for scientists to propose multibillion-dollar research efforts. Witness the superconducting supercollider, the Human Genome Project, the doubling of the National Science Foundation budget, and the space station among others. At such a rate of increase it is easy for requests for funding for science to exceed what even the most generous society can or will support. And if promised results and major discoveries are not forthcoming from large projects, society may soon become disillusioned and curtail future support. The potential discoverer can best serve science and society in this situation by concentrating on success in the form of discovery. The building of large projects for the sake of having a large project or for other profit is to be avoided. And once funded, a project must be made to produce the results for which it was designed, and more so, if possible.

In some large projects the effort by most individuals is not in science discovery per se. It may include planning, management, technology, even preparation of slick brochures. The doing of science may become something far removed from the making of discovery for most of the individuals involved.

Where does the discovery seeker go in such a world of science? To some extent that depends on the nature of one's interest, of course. One simple principle seems to hold generally, though. It is to try to become associated with the fresh new observations. That is where the discoveries are most likely. Try to work with the observations as early in their history as possible. Focus heavily on what those new observations may reveal. Of course, a substantial contribution of effort to the carrying out of the project may be necessary in order for the would-be discoverer to merit the opportunity to work with the data. That is only fair. But the focus on discovery and the data should never be lost or forgotten in the process.

If for some reason, a bound and determined discoverer on a large project cannot get access to the data, it is probably better for the individual to move elsewhere where observations are accessible.

Science may indeed stifle itself before its time, or it may be stifled by others before its time. Concentrating attention on observation and discovery, however, may be the best way for the individual to forestall and delay the stifling.

The Discoverers and the Do-It-Righters

DISCOVERY, in the sense I have used the term in this book, is not all there is to science. Discoverers tend to be at one end of the spectrum of styles in science. At another extreme are the do-it-righters. I choose these two terms as more appropriate than, say, *explorer, observer, synthesizer,* or *theoretician,* terms that have other connotations.

Discoverers tend to be entranced by novelty, by the thrill of knowing something before anyone else knows it, by the challenge of the unknown, and by the beauty of simplicity. Do-it-righters, on the other hand, are pleased by the order and thoroughness of a comprehensive explanation of a phenomenon. They seek the beauty of organization of science into its most concise and most elegant form. The discoverer is enchanted by the finding of a new concept or a new way to understand a phenomenon. The do-it-righter is less excited by the appearance of a basic concept but is disturbed by the loose ends that inevitably accompany a new discovery. The do-it-righter seeks a tidier world with more emphasis on the achievement of order than of revelation. The discoverer seeks the new paradigm. The do-it-righter tends toward the puzzle-solving side of science.

The world of science needs both types of scientists, of course. And it needs a full spectrum of those with intermediate interests and proclivities as well. In fact, not many scientists can be easily categorized as solely a discoverer or a do-it-righter. Most scientists combine the activities and interests of both types. Science would not function well if a clear-cut division existed.

Nevertheless, it would be naive to ignore this basic difference in the styles of science and scientists. This book is oriented, of course, toward the discoverer. It emphasizes the search for the novel and the basic. But there is no intent to minimize or downgrade the importance of the do-it-righter. In the eyes of the discoverer, the do-it-righter is an important component of science though not one working in the most exciting (for the discoverer) part of the subject. In the eyes of the do-it-righter, the discoverer has collected unconnected but not unrelated facts and missed the joy of seeing those facts assembled elegantly into a coherent picture.

Consider this straightforward example. As the geography of the bulk of the earth's surface was being explored by Europeans a few hundred years ago, explorers traveled to previously unvisited parts of the earth. Most became discoverers. They found new continents, new islands, new seas, new coastlines, new rivers, and new mountain ranges. It was a marvelous time in history for the explorer-discoverer. A great unknown (to Europeans) frontier was available and with modest effort discovery was almost assured.

In addition, at that time communication had advanced to the point where a less venturesome and nontraveling group of scholars could also play an important role. They were the cartographers. Cartographers mostly collected the observations of others and, like the theoretician or synthesizer of modern scientific data, attempted to assemble and interrelate that data in reasonable and realistic form; i.e., they made maps. Often, in doing so, they recognized new relationships or envisioned a whole not previously recognized and built a fresh perspective of the earth. In fact, although society in general and explorers, in particular, may not see it that way, cartographers and some others felt that, indeed, it was they who were making the big discoveries. And, indeed, sometimes they were, just as in modern science the do-it-righter may sometimes be the first to gain the important new insight.

Examples of discovering followed by do-it-righting can be found in almost any branch of science. Consider this one from the field of seismology. Early measurements of the seismic wave train generated by distant earthquakes revealed, among other waves, a train of slowly traveling waves of long duration and near-constant period. At first the nature of these waves was not understood. They seemed akin to elastic surface waves, but the duration and spectrum were not explained by application of existing theory to simple models of the earth. In an attempt to explain the discrepancy, some said the duration was a consequence of continuing disturbance at the source. Others said it was a consequence of scattering of the wave train by heterogeneities in the earth.

Eventually it was revealed by Ewing and Press that the wave train's appearance was largely a consequence of dispersion in a wave guide made of two highly contrasting materials, rock and water. Their explanation proved correct. The discovery of the basic principle involved was achieved.

The discovery left a lot of loose ends, however, because the earth's structure is much more complex than the simple model suggested. It is composed of not one but many different types of rock, each with different elastic properties. Eventually a more nearly complete theory was formulated by Pekeris and Haskell, to name just two, that permitted more realistic models of the earth to be used. With the new theoretical basis, computers now provide theoretical predictions for almost any situation. The subject has been "done right." The basic understanding of the phenomenon by discoverers was followed by masterful control of the subject by do-it-righters, and science made another firm step ahead.

For a description of what happens if a subject is "done right" before all the relevant discoveries are completed, see Chapter 3, "Overcoming the 'Terminal' Paper."

Big Science vs. Little Science, the Wrong Focus

OVER the last few decades, the style of conducting science has evolved in many ways, none more evident than the increasing fraction of effort and money directed to large projects. Once an activity characterized by the efforts of many individuals acting more or less independently, science now has a growing component that involves the coordinated efforts of teams of research scientists, technicians, managers, and others, each specializing in a particular part of an overall effort directed toward a single goal. Sometimes the goal is solution of a scientific problem, sometimes the operation of a facility for the use of many scientists each with a different problem. Such large projects are known individually and collectively as "big science."

The isolated independent investigator has not vanished from the scene by any means. There are many such individuals. They are growing in number and they remain a major and important component of science. This component is known collectively as "small science" or "little science," "little" because the scale of each separate effort is small even though the total effort involved may be comparable to, or much larger than, the "big science" fraction in any particular discipline.

In recent years, it has become fashionable in the scientific community to debate the issue of big science vs. little science. Should one or the other receive greater emphasis in terms of funding, organization, and attention and participation by scientists? The debate is stimulated by limitations on funding for science; by the proposing of more and more, larger and larger, costlier and costlier, scientific projects; by increasing numbers of scientists and institutions practicing small science; and by a variety of views on just how and why progress in science is made. The issue is of considerable interest to those seeking discovery, for the organizational structure of science clearly affects the opportunities available for discovery.

In many ways, the emphasis in the debate seems misplaced. For one thing, there is no clear boundary between big science and little science. A scientific project may involve any number of scientists—one, two, five, or two hundred. An expensive, elaborate, multistaffed facility may provide services for an individual who nevertheless is working on a problem in complete isolation except for use of the facility. There is a near-continuous spectrum of sizes and types of scientific projects, not the bimodal distribution implied by the two terms "big" and "little." Consequently, use of these terms is often inconsistent from one discussion to the next. Often only the extreme cases are discussed while the intermediate ones are ignored.

The term *big science,* for example, may refer only to huge multibillion-dollar projects, such as the superconducting supercollider, the Human Genome Project, or the manned exploration of Mars. Or it may include much less costly projects, such as operation of an oceanographic ship, a seismograph network, or an X-ray facility, that nevertheless require some coordinated efforts. Or big science might refer to any project involving more than a few scientists. The term "big science" is often used in debate without clear definition.

The debate is usually about whether, in the face of limited funding for science, big science should be supported if small science suffers in the process. Advocates of small science claim that it has produced the bulk of new ideas and advancement in science in the past and, hence, that continuing support is merited and of highest priority in the future. Advocates of big science claim that some branches of science have advanced to the point where the only way to obtain the key observations that relate to the major problems and opportunities of the science is through large, coordinated efforts. Both points of view may be challenged and supported.

The debate seems endless and the opposing sides irreconcilable. Yet the emphasis in the debate seems strangely misplaced. The issue is not whether big science or little science should be supported at the expense of the other. The answer to that question is clear. A spectrum of scientific projects of a variety of sizes should be supported. The shape of that spectrum, i.e., the distribution of sizes and kinds of projects, should be that which optimizes the production of science at that particular time in history. It should be easy for everyone to agree on that goal. The issue that requires debate, consideration, evaluation, and resolution is just what the shape of the spectrum, or more specifically the particular array of projects regardless of scale, should be in order to optimize scientific output for the benefit of society, practically and intellectually. That is the real issue and to obscure it with a terms like *big science vs. little science* seems misguided.

To state the foregoing is not to solve the problem, of course. There remains the difficult and nearly impossible task of deciding just what the optimum blend of science should be. But facing the real issue no matter how difficult is surely preferable to wasting effort and emotion on what is at best a secondary matter and at worst an idealized straw man. The ideal, practical solution to the main problem will likely never be fully achieved, and a continual process of readjustment and redirection is in order. That, in fact, is how we carry on today. We must strive to improve further. The following draw attention to some relevant supplementary points.

For one thing it seems clear that science should not evolve into an entitlement program for scientists. Science should not be a component of the welfare system. Scientists are among the brightest and most gifted members of society. Their role should be to contribute to the good of society, not to draw from, or become a burden on, society. Scientists do not merit support simply because they are scientists. They merit support because it appears they will produce something of benefit to the society that supports them, whether that benefit be practical or intellectual.

Nor should science be supported for reasons of partisan politics. If distribution of funding affects the geographical distribution of science, then the geographical distribution that most promotes the progress of science should be sought, not that which seems most palatable politically. The pork-barreling of science to the detriment of scientific progress is inexcusable at a time when society needs the best that science can offer. To put the matter in popular economic terms, it is increased productivity in science that we need and must seek.

To evaluate one scientific project in competition with another is a difficult task, one that most scientists are reluctant to undertake. It is especially difficult when the projects are in completely different branches of science. Yet it must be done. By using the wisest and most experienced judges, a reasonable and satisfactory, though not necessarily optimum, outcome should be achieved. Whether those judges should come entirely from the scientific sphere or partly from the scientific sphere and partly from the political or some other sphere is a complex matter dependent partly on the size and scope of the project. It seems evident, however, that experience with the process of discovery is a valuable component of the decision-making process and, hence, that experienced scientists must have a voice in such decisions.

It is also evident that, inasmuch as most scientists working in basic science are in small science projects, the majority of scientists are likely to favor small science over big science. So long as the proposition is put in that manner, most will act so as to defend the support available for small science. For this reason very large and costly projects are often guided by their leaders so that the key decisions go beyond the scientific community, where a one-person-one-vote decision would likely be negative, to a political level, where a different set of self-interests prevails.

The potential discoverer who proposes and defends an innovative new project must recognize the existence of the big science-little science debate in science and act so as to present that project in a light that permits and encourages a rational decision concerning support of that project. The best case can be made, of course, when the scientific potential of the project and its potential value to society are so overwhelming as to prevail over less relevant factors, such as the "size" of the science effort. The discoverer can enhance the prospects for discovery by seeking and selecting projects with such characteristics.

The Fundamental Conflict Between Bureaucracy and Science

In the modern world, most research in basic science is supported by public funds, directly or indirectly. There are other substantial sources in industry, in private foundations, in universities, and elsewhere, but the bulk of the support is government related. This relationship brings government bureaucracy into close association with science and bureaucrats in close connection with scientists. The relationship has an irregular history. There have been some notable successes and failures and a spectrum of efforts of intermediate levels of achievement.

The coupling of bureaucracy and science is a mismatch of sorts. Science is an activity with a major goal of finding something new. To maintain the status quo in scientific research is to fail. To overturn or revise a major section of science is to succeed. Continual upheaval and betterment are the characteristics of healthy science. Bureaucracy, on the other hand is generally geared to maintaining the status quo. Discovery, innovation, and creativity are not the goals of the bureaucracy. Boorstin, an outstanding author and perceptive observer of society, has written on bureaucracy in a broader sense than just its relation to science. At one point, in order to characterize bureaucracy he calls attention to a sign on the desk of a foreign civil servant reading "Never Do Anything for the First Time." It describes concisely the credo of the entrenched and intransigent bureaucrat. Such a sign is not likely to be found on the desk of a scientist—ever.

When government-supported science has thrived, then, how has it done so? The answer to that question is not simple, but one explanation is that the leaders on the government side in successful collaborations have managed, perhaps because of short tenure in government or an independent spirit on the part of an individual, not to become indoctrinated in the ways of the entrenched bureaucracy. In the upper echelons of the U.S. government science establishment, changes of personnel are frequent. With new blood entering from outside, a fresh and progressive attitude can be achieved and maintained in the bureaucratic organization.

At lower levels, where replacement and rotation through bureaucratic positions are less common, an occasional civil servant manages to maintain freshness, but many succumb to the temptation to minimize ripples, i.e., to forestall change. Yet change is the stuff of science! If bureaucracy of this sort thrives, science becomes mediocre.

It is at least partly because of bureaucratic forces that division among the scientific specialties becomes more pronounced and routine kinds of science prevail over more ambitious but also more risky kinds. A division of a government funding agency along disciplinary lines forces a corresponding division within the scientific community to some degree. An orderly and administratively well-run program of routine science entails less risk for the bureaucrat and draws less criticism from the scientific community, many of whom are engaged in routine science. But routine science is clearly not the best of science nor a sufficiently ambitious goal at this wonderful time in history when major discoveries seem available to those bold and daring enough to seek them.

The fundamental conflict between bureaucracy and science has been overcome in the past by the judicious leadership of special individuals in the bureaucracy or by the political savvy of leaders in the sciences. But the matter merits continuing vigilance and attention in the future. The would-be discoverer must recognize this situation and act so as to foster support for sound and inspired projects in the face of the basic conflict. Reason and good sense usually prevail, but the path may not be a smooth one. A would-be discoverer may find that charting a path through the bureaucracy may be as important a part of the discovery process as charting a course through the structure of science is.

The Joys and Perils of Success

SUCCESS in scientific discovery is rewarding, most of the time. In addition to the private joy of being the first in history to know a particular thing, discovery brings other benefits. Science is generous in its honors in recognition of the special efforts that lead to discovery. Citations, medals, honorary degrees, election to academies, prizes, election to fellowship or official position in scientific societies, salary increases, promotions, career changes, and grants may result from accomplishments that often seem at least as much a consequence of serendipity as brilliant effort by the recipient. Honors that once seemed trivial or superficial to hard-driving young scientists suddenly take on new meaning as those scientists' careers mature and they become recipients. Recognition by one's colleagues is indeed satisfying. There is no need to be so modest as to downplay that fact of life.

Sometimes deserved recognition is, sadly, not forthcoming. An important discovery may not be recognized until after the discoverer has passed away. That was the case for Wegener.

And recognition may be unduly delayed. Morley, for example, independently postulated the same mechanism to explain the magnetic anomalies at spreading centers as Vine and Matthews did. Through an unfortunate set of circumstances, Morley's paper was rejected for publication. Fortunately, the case has now become so well known that general recognition of Morley's contribution is in effect. And the comment of the reviewer who recommended rejection of the paper by noting that the idea was one that should be discussed at cocktail parties but not published in a scientific journal has become a warning to all subsequent reviewers. Nevertheless, and in spite of occasional flaws and inequities, scientific discovery normally brings rewards and satisfaction to the discoverer.

Success in science, as in other endeavors, is not without its perils, however. There is some of the game of king of the hill in science. Scientists who excel and outdo their colleagues will receive accolades. But they and their work may also become the target of increasingly severe scrutiny and painstaking critique. Many would like to displace the current leader. Such a process is partly to the good. Science cannot afford to be misled by its leaders, and those who rise into a position of leadership must expect the highest level of criticism and should feel pressure to maintain or surpass that level of excellence.

But the process can also work to the detriment of science. Those who have achieved superior results through unconventional means may find themselves reined in and held to conventional behavior by reviewers envious of the achievements. Such restraint is detrimental to science because it affects most strongly those imaginative leaders who are capable of providing science with its finest advances. Leaders of large projects requiring high levels of funding must also anticipate extraordinary attack and criticism. Such criticism may be well founded in some cases but a consequence of envy or an attitude of divide and conquer in others. To gain the lead is to become a special target of criticism by those seeking the lead. In this regard science is little different from other walks of life. The phenomenon is not unusual, but the young scientist should not be so naive as to think it does not exist.

Youth and Age

THAT major discoveries are made only by young scientists is a popular notion, popular at least among the public. One sometimes hears it stated that a scientist who has not made a discovery by the midtwenties has missed the opportunity and should be channeled into a nonresearch position.

Scientists recognize that view is in error. Many major discoveries have indeed been made by bright, young scientists and science must always maintain a structure that permits a young upstart to break through to upper echelons. But many important discoveries have been made by older scientists as well. Those who have passed the midtwenties, or even the midfifties or midseventies, need not give up hope. Their greatest discovery may still be ahead.

Certainly for earth science there is a record of discovery that involves scientists of almost every age. When they published their major contribution to the development of plate tectonics, the ages of these key contributors were as follows: Alfred Wegener (theory of continental drift) 42; Harry Hess (concept of sea floor spreading) 56; Fred Vine (mechanism for generation of marine magnetic anomalies) 24; J. Tuzo Wilson (transform fault hypothesis) 57; Jason Morgan (geometry and pattern of motion of plates) 32; John Dewey (integration of geology with plate tectonic concept) 33; Donald Turcotte (dynamics of interior) 37; Allan Cox (reversals of earth's magnetic field) 38; Walter Elsasser (origin of magnetic field and tectonic models) 64.

These data, and others, suggest a bias in favor of younger scientists. The young are inclined to seize the opportunity and make the most of it. But there are sufficient major contributions by older scientists, in fact by scientists of almost all ages, that no age group can be written off with regard to discovery.

The fact of some major discovery by older scientists suggests that their lesser rate of discovery on the average is not, as some have implied, a consequence of some poorly understood organic change that affects the brain. A more likely explanation is that older scientists have become more heavily involved in time-consuming tasks that limit the fraction of their effort that can be directed to discovery. Administration, teaching, and management do not burden the young so much as the old. And tenure, financial security, and demands of family may dull the cutting edge once held by a youthful scientist. But the effects of over-indoctrination, administrative diversion, and the mellowing of

age can be overcome by those with sufficient intensity of purpose.

In any case, the fact remains that discovery has been, and
hence can be, made by scientists of any age. Indeed, we might
ask if society's capacity for discovery could be enhanced by help-
ing the most innovative of our young scientists to avoid the
stifling duties that normally accompany senior status. In any
case, the message for scientists of all ages is heartening. The
capacity for discovery need not diminish as age increases. Age
may be a detriment, but it is not an excuse.

There Is Only One Earth

THE style of conducting science varies from one branch of science to the next for a variety of reasons. Some branches are old
and mature; some are new and fertile. Some are a maze of plen-
tiful observations, in others observations are sparse indeed. Some
are concerned with basic, widely applicable laws; others, with
the application of those laws to complex subjects. Physics, for
example, is a basic science whose principles are applicable
throughout all of science. Geology is not a basic science in that
sense; it is instead the application of basic scientific principles
to understanding of the earth. Physics is often reductionist,
attempting to understand thoroughly a simple or limited component of nature. Geology often seeks to be reductionist but, in
so doing, is moderated by the need to understand the earth in all
its complexity, not merely a single or selected component. There
is another important difference. Physicists often study the nature of objects (atoms for example) that exist in innumerable
quantities. Geologists study one body, the earth.

Physicists, for example, operate on the basis that all atoms of
a particular substance in the same state are the same. Thus
there can be a general model for the atom and it is assumed that
all such atoms of that substance will behave according to that
single model. Either it is assumed that this is so or it is demonstrated by observation of the collective behavior of many such
atoms. It is not demonstrated by observation of single atoms that
this is the case. (Likely the assumption is correct. If it is not, the
science of physics is in for a major shake-up. As a digression,
however, think how exciting it would be if subtle differences in
individual atoms could be observed!) The point of interest here

is that, because of the huge numbers of objects involved, physicists develop models of processes involving atoms and the models can be applied widely. That is virtually the only way to proceed in that branch of science.

Carrying over that reductionist style of science blindly to other scientific disciplines may not, however, be the best way to proceed in those sciences. Consider the case of geology. A geologist wishing to understand mountain ranges and following the style of the physicist might decide to study one mountain range in detail and apply the results to other mountain ranges, assuming they are all similar.

In fact, to some extent early geology proceeded in this manner. The Alps, for example, conveniently located in Europe, were studied in detail, their processes of formation deduced, and the resulting model was applied to mountain ranges elsewhere. This approach has some merit. It was particularly useful in the early stages of geology when access to remote mountain ranges was difficult or impossible.

Now, however, the science has advanced beyond the point where such a simple model is adequate. Mountain ranges are not alike in the sense that atoms are, or seem to be. There are important differences. Some mountain ranges have little similarity to others. Of course, it is always useful to seek similarities from one range to the next, but now it is time to study differences as well. And it is feasible to do so because transportation has so greatly improved that almost all mountain ranges are accessible to the geologist who chooses to visit them.

In this situation, it does not make sense to strive to develop a general model beyond a certain point, for each mountain range can be studied and understood in its own right, and that is the understanding we seek. We want to know how the Alps were formed, and how the Himalayas were formed, and how the Andes were formed, and so on for all the ranges of the world. Of course, we want to know similarities from one range to another, and our models are surely helpful in learning about ancient ranges for which only fragmentary evidence is found, but our ultimate goal is to understand mountain ranges. The goal is not so much to make an elegant model that is some sort of approximation to those mountains. Unless that model helps us to understand better the real mountains of the earth (or some other planet) it is not the basic need. In short, there is only one earth that we need to understand in geology, and our efforts should be focused on that subject. We need to be concerned with the creation of elegant models or elaborate processes only to the extent that they help in that understanding, not for their own sake.

The researcher in earth science can improve the opportunities for discovery by capitalizing upon newfound capability for studying the entire earth or remote parts of it in ways never before possible. In recent years, scientists have explored Antarctica, the depths of the sea, the rift valleys of Africa, even the moon. Satellites have produced global maps of gravity and various types of images of remote areas. Aircraft and ships have surveyed the magnetic field. It is not unreasonable today to contemplate comprehensive seismic studies of the continental crust that will reveal the third dimension of geology everywhere. Comprehensive geochemical surveys can be conducted on a global basis.

There is indeed only one earth to study and that earth is figuratively shrinking as society develops. Opportunities for earth scientists abound in this new era. They should be capitalized upon and greeted with pleasure by earth scientists for they will almost certainly produce the comprehensive understanding of earth that we seek.

How to Recognize an Important Contribution to Science

IN the modern world of science, a bewildering array of new scientific results is added continually. History demonstrates that only a fraction of this material will have lasting impact on the science. Much of it will lie forever unutilized on library shelves. How can one recognize just which contributions will have staying power; i.e., which are of special importance? This question is an important one for all scientists and it is a critical one for the would-be discoverer who is trying to gauge the flow of the milieu.

Of course, the value of any particular scientific contribution can be judged with certainty or finality only from the perspective of history. That judgment may occur a decade, or many decades, after its appearance. But the practicing scientist cannot wait that long and must have a prompt evaluation, even though it may be tentative.

There are many methods and criteria for early evaluation of a new scientific contribution. All are imperfect and most give very questionable results. One stands out in reliability above all others. It is based on observation of whether other scientists readjust their activities and their lives as a consequence of learning about the new result. Sometimes a scientific paper will present a new idea or a new observation or a new technique, and many scientists throughout the world will change their activities significantly in order to exploit the new information or the new technique. Such a response represents strong endorsement by the scientific community and likely means that the paper will have lasting impact.

Contrast this criterion with a less reliable one. One often hears a paper or the author described as "clever." And indeed the work may demonstrate remarkable ingenuity, ability, and effort on the part of the author. But the subject may be poorly chosen and of little consequence to the flow of the science. Thus other scientists, though struck with admiration, find nothing that leads them, consciously or subconsciously, to act differently than they would have in the absence of the paper. Such a paper, even though "cleverly done" is probably not an important contribution to science.

In a related category are those papers that introduce a sophisticated theory or technique without demonstrating the worth of the method to the science. Without the demonstration, the value is not evident and the paper may well be forgotten. Perhaps such a consequence is natural. The lack of demonstration may mean that even the author could not visualize any possible impacts of the paper on the flow of science.

There are some surprises, of course. The utility and worth of a paper that initially seemed inconsequential may be discovered much later to the surprise of all. In such cases there is a delayed response by the scientific community to the paper. Although there are important examples of this phenomenon, such cases are the exception. The best method of evaluating the importance of a paper shortly after it appears is by gauging the number of scientists who do something differently because of it and soon after it appears. And by doing something differently, I mean something beyond simply citing the paper in the literature. Perhaps new experiments are tried in the laboratory, a new research project is initiated, or special trips are taken to observe the phenomena of interest.

Citation indices have become a well-known basis for evaluation of papers a few years after publication. This basis has some merit but less so than the observation of actual change in scientific activity by individuals. To cite, in fact, is but a mild form of the kind of activity change referred to above.

There are many other imperfect ways of judging the merit of a new contribution to science. Appearance in the news media is one. Often, however, such appearance is more a consequence of the journalist's idea of what will make a story for the general public than of a well-considered evaluation of the result's significance in science.

Honors to the author, granting of funds to conduct research based on the paper, and republication in semiprofessional journals servicing a broad segment of the scientific community are additional, but also imperfect, factors on which judgment may be based. None, however, is as telling or as accurate as that based on change in not only thought but also action by the scientific community.

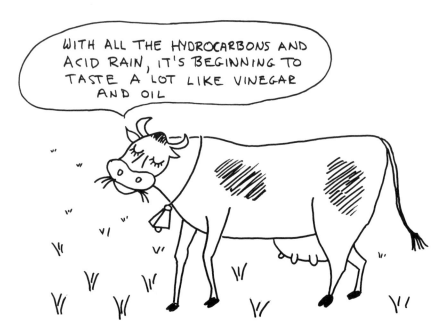

How to Recognize That You Have Made an Important Discovery

As described in the previous section, the ability to recognize a significant contribution to science by someone else is vitally important for a scientist working at the forefront of the field. Of at least equal importance is a scientist's capability to recognize that he or she has made an important discovery. That fact is not always immediately evident to the discoverer. And whereas a contribution by others is judged only after the information has been made public, the individual scientist would like to make an evaluation of the discovery before it becomes known to the public.

On this more immediate time scale, the task of evaluation is even more difficult and even less certain. It is complicated because an evaluation made by the originator, sometimes while the work is proceeding, can easily be colored by that individual's enthusiasm, hopes, and dreams and those of fellow participants. It is difficult for anyone to be fully objective about one's own contribution.

There is, however, one effect that is normally a powerful sign of important discovery. In a typical scientific project, data are collected and an effort is made to organize the observations according to some new concept, or idea, or theory. The scientist must be concerned that his or her new ideas fit well not only with the observations of the project but also with all other observations familiar to him or her. If a new concept is found that fits all the data that he or she is aware of, the investigator is, and should be, highly encouraged.

Next comes the telling step that can clarify the importance of the contribution. If the scientist gradually begins to discover new or previously unrecognized data, often of kinds with which he or she has no prior familiarity, that fit the ideas based independently on the initial set of data, the discovery is likely an important one. And the more diverse and numerous the compatible but previously unknown observations are, the greater the importance and the greater the certainty of the importance of the discovery.

That is the essence of this guideline. The falling into place of previously unknown and unsuspected data of various kinds within a newly proposed hypothesis should impart great confidence in the ultimate worth of that hypothesis.

There is an intangible side to the story as well. Once things start to fall into place in the manner described above, the discoverer, particularly one strongly guided by intuition, knows that he or she has found the target or hit the jackpot. A certain sense of elation follows and he or she acquires the confidence to defend the story against the critical attacks of others.

Of course, no one is infallible and even one so elated may occasionally be wrong. But such occasions are rare. More often the self-critical scientist who read the telltale signs of discovery in the making will be able to convince himself or herself of the achievement, and do so correctly, long before the less appropriately informed scientific community as a whole recognizes the discovery.

Major Discoveries Are Not Made Democratically

WARNING: The political idealist may feel uncomfortable with this section. So will the egalitarian and the antielitist. Nevertheless, facts must be faced. Science is an activity of the elite and of those striving to be elite. Scientific discovery is an activity that relies heavily on the brains of special individuals. A unique event happens to an individual on the occasion of discovery. It makes him or her a member of an elite. The nature of discovery is such that there can be no alternative. If scientific discovery is to be optimized, the system of governing and managing scientific activity must be devised to tolerate and encourage this form of elitism.

Democracy is surely the finest form of government yet devised. It can be practiced appropriately on a wide variety of scales and in many types of organizations. Democracy is a remarkably versatile and basically fair style of governing. Nevertheless, the chance of major scientific discovery is usually not optimized by operating democratically.

Discovery is commonly the product of inspiration and insight on the part of a gifted individual placed in a favorable situation. It is the result of that individual's brilliance, and good fortune, and willingness to depart from the norm, i.e., to go in a direction *different* from that of the group. Discovery is not often the product of a voting body. A voting body may act with great wisdom. It steers a course between the extremes. It will, therefore, avoid the great pitfall. But it will also avoid the favorable extreme as well. A voting body is rarely if ever capable of the brilliant master stroke that reveals the unknown.

This conflict between democracy and the process of discovery is fundamental. Discovery demands breaking away from the mainstream. Democracy is a way to determine, and follow, the mainstream. Discovery hinges on the decisions and performance of an individual; democracy is a collective process. The two are incompatible. Except in the most unusual circumstances, democracy cannot make the optimum decisions for discovery.

This principle is well known and highly respected in universities. Most modern universities have ways for faculty members to participate in direction of the university. There are faculty meetings, councils of representatives, senates, committees, etc. Such groups consider a variety of matters and usually resolve them by democratic means. The board of trustees that governs the university operates in similar manner. So do various groups of students.

With rare exceptions, none of these bodies, however, would

dare to prescribe how an individual faculty member should conduct research or even what the topic of the research should be. It is widely recognized that freedom for the individual to set one's own course to discovery is critical to the process. Such a policy is an important component of academic freedom.

One can cite examples in which attempts are made to employ democratic means in the guidance of science. Perhaps the most prominent example is found in the government science advisory structure. Often a committee of experts is assembled and asked to recommend future research on some particular topic. Various ideas are expressed and controversy arises. The controversy is resolved by democratic vote or compromise. The result is never bad, usually good, but never excellent. As one scientist put it, "The report that emerges consists of everyone's second choice." That is an apt description. It is not the way to major discovery.

What saves the government advisory system is that committee recommendations are used mostly to generate research funding. Once the funding is available, an individual researcher can propose as a research project, a "first choice." First choices are often sufficiently appealing that they slip through the system and discoveries result.

SEVEN

The Inside Story of One Discovery

T HIS chapter differs from all others of this book. It is an attempt to set down and interrelate, with some thoroughness, the series of events and the evolution of thought that led to a particular discovery in earth science. It is, in other words, a case history of a discovery. The history follows the discovery from preliminaries through the stage of hard work, observation, careful analysis, and evaluation; then through the climactic stage that included the moment of enlightenment; and finally through the follow-up stage when the early interaction of the discovery with other parts of science was gradually revealed. It describes attitudes, strategies, decisions, and associations. It illustrates how application of the principles of certain of the guidelines of other chapters combined with some very good fortune to produce the discovery. I would not like to claim that the process of discovery in this one example is identical to that process in all cases of discovery, but on the other hand, there are clearly elements and patterns that are common to many other scientific discoveries of both greater and lesser significance.

The example is the story of discovery of the downgoing slab of lithosphere that is the key element in the process of subduction. When I use the term *the discovery* in this chapter, it always means that particular discovery. We now know, but did not know before the discovery, that the subduction process takes place at the sites of the great physiographic arcs such as Japan, the Andes, the East Indies, the Himalayas, or Tonga where the discovery was made. The arcs are the places where the plates of plate tectonics converge and where one plate plunges beneath the other, carrying near-surface material into the interior. At such places, mountain ranges and plateaus are built, deep sea trenches are formed, explosive volcanism and the greatest earthquakes occur, and continents collide. The convergent zones are the sites of much of the action of global tectonics. The two plates of lithosphere are the key elements and that they converge and interact to cause these phenomena as one plunges beneath the other is the essence of the discovery.

Though the subject was speculated upon earlier by some, sometimes with remarkable vision, at the time our story begins, the arcs and their accompanying processes were not well understood. Their nature was neither agreed upon by earth scientists nor integrated into the global tectonic picture at that time. The term *subduction* was not used. The concept of plate tectonics was not known.

The discovery was an important one. It was a critical element in development of understanding of the subduction process and hence in construction of the concept of plate tectonics. It was not, however, of the magnitude of the discoveries of great scientific paradigms or great new phenomena such as, say, the finding of radioactivity, DNA, relativity, evolution, or plate tectonics. Most records and analyses of the discovery process concern those grand accomplishments. This account concerns a discovery of lesser, but certainly nontrivial, importance. As such, the account may be of interest to those who wish to compare the pattern of a modest discovery with that for a more grandiose achievement. Such a comparison and evaluation are not the prime purpose of this account, however. That purpose is instead to see a particular discovery in the light of the guidelines of this book.

The discovery selected as an example is one in which I was heavily involved. If the reader finds the choice too author centered, I apologize. For the initial draft of this book I tried to avoid the use of examples in which I was a key figure. However, readers of that draft encouraged the addition of one thorough and well-elaborated example of a particular discovery. Such an account seems best based on personal experience. What follows is as nearly complete and accurate as it can be, subject to limitations of space and memory.

In the preface, I related the story of how a football injury, and fate, put me in contact with Professor Maurice Ewing, the Columbia University geophysicist who became my adviser, my mentor, and eventually my colleague (or I his). By joining Ewing, I accomplished inadvertently what a guideline in Chapter 3 recommends, i.e., to undertake graduate study under a leader of the field.

Some of Ewing's broad-ranging and visionary activities set the stage for this discovery. He founded the Lamont-Doherty Geological Observatory, a maverick organization that strongly reflected Ewing's imaginative style and his strong roots in fundamentals and emphasis on observation. With his student, and later colleague, Frank Press (who would become President Carter's science adviser), he began a program at Lamont-Doherty in earthquake seismology that was hard driving, innovative, and ever alert to new opportunities (see Chapter 2). Later, when I succeeded Press as head of that program, I inherited not only the facilities and the organization but also that style and attitude.

In the early days Ewing taught by example and participated heavily in seismological research. One study by Ewing and others was not the most notable of his many scientific contributions, but almost as a by-product it produced a piece of information that would later become important to the discovery described here. During the late 1940s and early 1950s, Ewing was interested in earthquake-generated waterborne sound. Consequently, he studied high-frequency seismic waves traveling from earthquakes in the West Indies across the western Atlantic to the Lamont station near New York City. The travel path was largely oceanic. In addition to the waterborne sound (the T phase of seismologists), Ewing found unusual high-frequency phases that had traveled through the uppermost and solid mantle as compressional and shear waves. It was a surprising observation. There had to be a special wave guide that channeled the high-frequency waves for long distances with little attenuation. As a close observer but not a participant in that effort, I was well aware of those results. A particular part of that study of the late 1940s, the secondary part having to do with the propagation of high-frequency shear waves in the upper mantle, would later be important to the discovery of the mid-1960s.

Another critical piece of information arose in a graduate course that reflected Ewing's interest in a broad spectrum of topics in geophysics. One topic was seismology, a subject in which the earth's interior was divided into crust, mantle, and core on the basis of seismic wave propagation, i.e., elastic phenomena. And then there were the topics of gravity and geodesy in which the uppermost portion of the same earth was divided into lithosphere and asthenosphere on the basis of rheological behavior following the style of Barrell, Chamberlain, and Daly. At the time it puzzled me that two classification schemes covering the same parts of the earth were entirely unrelated (see Chapter 5). Moreover, it seemed that little attention was given by scientists of that era to the need to make that relationship (see Chapter 2). The convenience of the multiple classification schemes may have produced complacency (see Chapter 5). And so it was satisfying that the way they could be related was revealed as part of the discovery that was to come.

Ewing had yet another effect on the processes that led to the discovery, in this case because of his policy of including study of a wide variety of earth phenomena within the program of his small but rapidly growing organization (see Chapter 2). He encouraged scientists at Lamont to pursue the topics of geomagnetism and paleomagnetism, among others. Those efforts eventually led Lamont into the plate tectonics revolution. And, among other things, workers in those disciplines influenced activities in the Lamont seismology program so as to affect the discovery. Lynn Sykes, a former graduate student of mine with exceptional talent, was stimulated by the Lamont work in geomagnetism related to sea floor spreading. As a consequence, he produced in the mid-1960s a key study of earthquake focal mechanisms. Sykes's study supported Wilson's ideas on transform faulting and gave stature to the sea floor spreading concept at a critical point in its development. Sykes's success and his enthusiasm for the new tectonic ideas had an influence on other seismologists and hence on the discovery.

Lamont's aggressive program in seismology had a strong observational slant that led, among other things, to the first seismograph on the moon and to an unusual observatory in a deep mine in New Jersey. The mine was chosen especially for operation of the low-frequency seismographs that were Lamont's specialty. However, another exceptional graduate student, Bryan Isacks, elected not to follow the crowd (see Chapter 2) and initiated a study there on waves at the opposite, high-frequency end of the spectrum. As part of that study, Isacks in the early 1960s studied waves like those investigated earlier by Ewing, i.e., the high-frequency shear waves traveling in the upper mantle between the West Indies and the New York-New Jersey area. Isacks, partly as a result of those efforts and that experience, would later become a major factor in the discovery.

Events outside Lamont were also important to the discovery. During the early 1960s, the international scientific community was engaged in the Upper Mantle Project. This project was a spur to scientists to work on this poorly known part of the earth, the upper 1000 km or so, and a stimulus for funding of the separate national or multinational efforts that were coordinated under the project. The discovery was, as we shall see, partly a consequence of efforts carried out under the Upper Mantle Project.

The preceding paragraphs of this chapter describe various people, activities, and events of the 1940s, 1950s, and 1960s that at the time seemed loosely related at best, but all would come together, directly or indirectly, to be a part of the process that led to the discovery. Let us now turn to the principal stream of events that culminated in the discovery. I shall draw on the foregoing topics as they become a part of the story.

During the early and mid-1950s, I was engaged in, and dedicated to, basic science, investigating the fundamentals of seismic wave propagation and using that information in exploration of the earth's interior. I made some discoveries during that period that were solid contributions to the science but that had limited impact beyond inner seismological circles. They were seismology for seismologists. In the late 1950s, as a consequence of discovery of a previously unobserved seismic wave generated by a buried nuclear explosion, I was drawn heavily into the technical aspects of political negotiations for a nuclear test ban treaty. Basic science was deferred as the heady and more urgent politically related science took precedence. (Now, after more than thirty years of political negotiations, and no treaty, the matter does not seem quite so urgent to me as it did then!) By the early 1960s, however, I had become weary of, and somewhat disillusioned with, applied scientific endeavors that were designed to affect the treaty negotiations but that also forced the scientist more and more into the political sphere. An international treaty is primarily a political matter; science plays a supporting role and political considerations are primary. And so it should be. But my personal interests were primarily scientific. I decided, therefore, to move into a new activity, one with the prospect of a substantial scientific discovery.

This well-defined and conscious shift in emphasis provided a special opportunity. A strategy with discovery as the primary goal could be used. I was in a position to choose a new project and was not hard pressed for time in doing so. In retrospect, the decision that resulted was a sound one, partly because of good luck, of course, but partly also because of reasoning in the style described in Chapters 2 and 3. I consciously spent long and hard thought on the choice of a topic and eventually decided that an observational study of deep earthquakes was in order. Deep earthquakes were prominent geological events. It seemed that understanding of them had to be important. I had never studied deep earthquakes before. However, the topic was not receiving much attention by other seismologists, particularly U.S. seismologists, at the time (see Chapter 2). And the understanding of deep earthquakes was in such a primitive state that it seemed the subject probably offered exceptional opportunity. We explored the matter in a graduate seminar at Lamont. At that time deep earthquakes (i.e., earthquakes whose foci are below the crust—where most earthquake foci are located—and sometimes at depths as great as 700 km) were recognized, and they were known from early Japanese studies to occur along dipping zones associated with island arcs. Little more was known. However, some things we now know to be incorrect were assumed with little or no basis in observation.

For example, it was thought, or assumed without great thought,

that deep earthquakes occur where they occur because of unusual movements or stresses in the rocks there. That was reasonable enough. But the rocks at those places were also thought
to be no different than rocks elsewhere in the mantle at the same
depth. It was assumed, in other words, that there were no lateral
variations in the mantle even at the places where the deep earthquakes took place. Such thinking was conditioned on the prevalent idea of that time that the earth's interior consisted of con-
centric, nearly spherical shells without lateral variation. That
generalization had a basis in observation. Seismic wave travel
times are largely a function of distance and not location on the
earth. Thus the earth's interior cannot vary wildly from place to
place. But the generalization obscured the fact that not all parts
of the earth had been carefully observed so as to test the concept
thoroughly with regard to small or modest variations. And even
if that deficiency in observation had been recognized, it could
not have been fully remedied. To make such comprehensive observations everywhere is a huge task, impossible in that era and
beyond capability even at present. Instead the time was ripe for
selective new observations and for a burst of intuition on just
where to make those observations.

At some later time in the study, and before the moment of
enlightenment, I had the hunch (see Chapter 2) that the rocks
where the deep earthquakes occurred might somehow be anomalous in some way. But as the field effort began, there was no
proper hypothesis to be tested, and no hypothetical model was
proposed for testing in the formal style of the so-called scientific
method. There was merely the plausible idea that something
might be learned by making some new observations of the phenomenon and of the earth in the vicinity of the phenomenon.

I next tried to assemble the elements of a project that would
observe deep earthquakes with some thoroughness. The key element was recruitment of a young scientist who could devote full
time to the project. (I had other time-consuming continuing
responsibilities.) My first choice for this position, and in retrospect it was an inspired one, was Bryan Isacks. Bryan had recently completed his doctorate. He had exceptional ability, including a strong intuitive sense for science, training in both
physics and geology, and appropriate and relevant experience
with instrumentation and analysis from his field studies in the

mine. He was enthusiastic, determined, eager to see and explore the earth, and anxious to make a contribution to science. It was my good fortune, indeed, when Bryan joined the nascent project.

In planning the project, we soon made the rather straightforward decision to operate a network of moderately high-frequency seismographs in an area surrounding a deep earthquake zone. But where? We wanted a site with ample deep earthquake activity and one where operation of the network could be managed logistically. After a global search, two sites rated far more highly than others. One was in South America along the Andes tectonic belt, the other in the Tonga-Fiji region of the South Pacific. In either case we had to face the challenge of operating the network in a region that was foreign and not well known to us. Initially I preferred the South American site because we had contacts there that would make the logistics easier. Bryan leaned toward the Pacific site because of the greater frequency of deep shocks there. We debated this matter for some time, but when some prospects for logistical support in the Pacific developed we agreed on that site because of its potential to produce greater quantities of data in a finite interval of time. In retrospect this was a key decision and it was made correctly because, in the style recommended in this book (see Chapter 3), we put the emphasis on accumulation of new observations.

We were granted funding for the project by the National Science Foundation (NSF). The timing was excellent because NSF was looking favorably at projects directed toward study of this part of the earth as a result of stimulation by the international Upper Mantle Project, a fact of which I was aware because of prior service on NSF committees. Nevertheless, it required some courage by NSF officials to grant funds for a project that might have been criticized by irresponsible politicians as a boondoggle, because it would operate in a locale that Hollywood might portray as a South Pacific paradise. The NSF leaders acted with a vision and a level of confidence that was not necessarily in the bureaucratic tradition (see Chapter 6). Any such apprehension soon disappeared. The project was not a boondoggle. In fact, in the history of NSF published in 1976, the Tonga-Fiji deep earthquake project was the first of six studies selected and cited as examples of NSF successes.

Fieldwork began in late 1964. Continuous operation of a net-

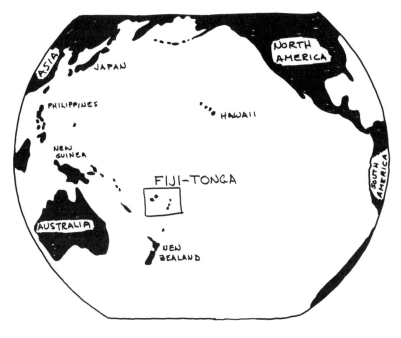

Figure 1

work of seismographs on various islands in Tonga and Fiji (figure 1) was the goal (figures 2 and 3). The installation and operation of delicate instruments on what were remote and actually less than paradisiacal islands was a difficult and often onerous task. But it was accomplished, largely through the imagination, perseverance, and dedication of Isacks. He benefited from the cooperation, support, and interest of others, including the islanders, for many of whom the activities seemed strange indeed. Bryan spent well over a year during 1964–65 in the region. He overcame a variety of problems, and eventually the network produced data as planned.

As the data began to come in, Bryan, who was the first to see them (see Chapter 8), was continually alert for any sign that the seismic zone was somehow different from its surroundings. We hoped for a detectable effect, probably in the form of a difference in velocity, but were concerned that such a velocity effect might be small and obscured by errors in location of the earthquake foci. It eventually turned out, to our delight, that the earth was

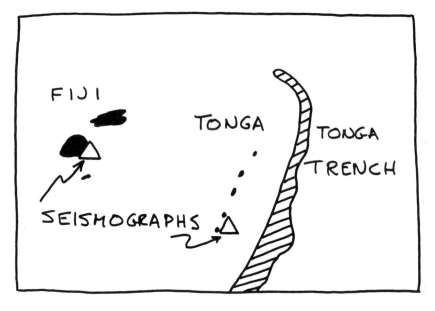

Figure 2

good to us, much better than we had ever hoped or anticipated. There was a velocity difference of a few percent and it could be detected. It was some time, however, before that effect was resolved or even given much attention. Something bigger was in store. From some of the early data, Bryan quickly recognized that there was a huge effect in attenuation that far outstripped anything we had dreamed of. The amplitudes of seismic waves traveling up the inclined seismic zone to Tonga were sometimes more than *three orders of magnitude* larger than those traveling a comparable but aseismic path to Fiji (figure 4). The differences in velocity were secondary. The differences in attenuation were predominant and astonishing. It was a startling result, and we knew, or at least suspected, that we were on to something important. But what? We had to develop some understanding of the effect as it related to other earth features and phenomena to make it meaningful.

It was many months before we hit upon the full meaning of those observations. Meanwhile, new earthquakes occurred and new observations reinforced and expanded the earlier ones, dem-

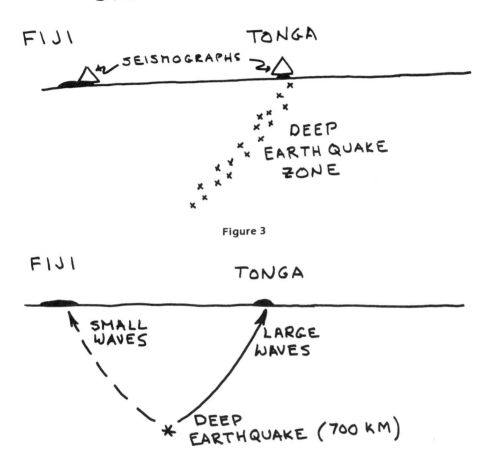

Figure 3

Figure 4

onstrating clearly that an inclined zone of very low attenuation (and slightly high velocity) enclosed the dipping zone of earthquake foci and included a limited portion of adjoining mantle as well (figure 5). We pondered the matter, but the full meaning of the observations escaped us for a time that seems embarrassingly long in retrospect.

Eventually the modern and now widely accepted interpreta-

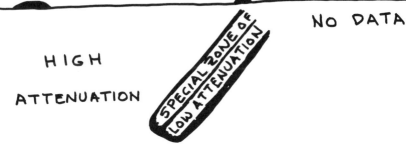

Figure 5

tion occurred to us when we considered the observations from Tonga-Fiji along with two additional pieces of information. Before the moment of enlightenment those two kinds of information had no, or at best a tenuous, relation to the deep earthquake story. One was the previous work by Ewing and others (including Isacks) on high-frequency waves in the shallow mantle of the western Atlantic. The other was the kind of thinking that had come to us from those who were excitedly pursuing the new topic of sea floor spreading. We were influenced by the proposers of the sea-floor-spreading hypothesis, by the geomagnetics specialists at Lamont who were busy using magnetic anomalies at sea to demonstrate the spreading, and by Lynn Sykes whose studies of earthquakes were critical to establishment of the nature of spreading as postulated by Tuzo Wilson.

At that time, as a consequence of preliminary success of the sea-floor-spreading theory, this new school of earth scientists faced an enigma. If the sea floor spread, and new surface area was created at the great rifts or spreading centers, was the earth expanding to accommodate the new surface area? Or were parts of the surface being destroyed elsewhere at a rate that balanced the creation of new sea floor? Some proposed that earth was indeed expanding. Some proposed that surface material was descending beneath the continents, some at the sites of trenches and island arcs, and some at widely distributed unspecified localities in an unspecified manner. Certain of these speculations

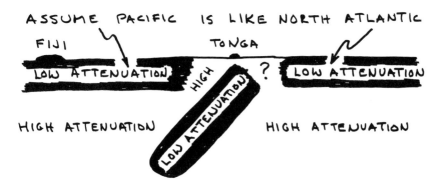

Figure 6

would turn out to be correct to a degree, and some early specula-
tors were insightful, but at the time no one knew for sure just
how or where the surface material went down, or even if it did.
Nevertheless, the enigma was widely known.

Then the great moment of the discovery, what some have
described as the "Eureka phenomenon," arrived. The setting was
my office at the Lamont Observatory. Bryan and I sat at a blackboard where I had drawn a cross-section through the Tonga-Fiji
area (figure 5). It showed, in simple fashion, the deep seismic
zone that exhibited the anomalous seismic wave propagation. It
showed no detail for the shallow mantle of the region outside our
seismic network in the Tonga-Fiji area. In particular, we had no
information on the shallow mantle east of Tonga, that is, east of
where the west-dipping seismic zone lay near the surface.

Recalling the unusually efficient propagation of high-frequency shear waves over Atlantic paths between the West Indies
and Lamont, I said, "The efficient shear wave propagation in the
inclined seismic zone of Tonga-Fiji is something like shallow
horizontal shear wave propagation in the western Atlantic. Why
don't we assume that shallow horizontal propagation in the Pacific mantle is also similar? Then we could draw it this way." And
I sketched figure 6 and then drew the now familiar picture of the
slab that is horizontal beneath normal sea floor and that bends
downward and descends in island arcs (figure 7).

Almost before I had completed the picture, Bryan, conscious
of the developing sea-floor-spreading story and the accompanying enigma, said, "Of course. It's underthrust!" How simple. How

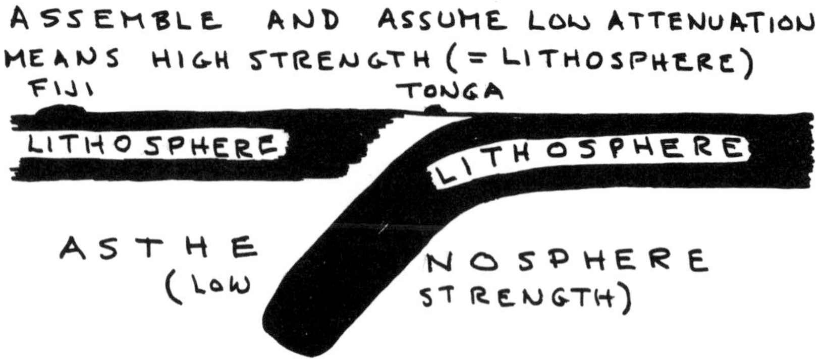

ASSEMBLE AND ASSUME LOW ATTENUATION
MEANS HIGH STRENGTH (= LITHOSPHERE)
FIJI   TONGA

LITHOSPHERE   LITHOSPHERE

ASTHE
(LOW   NOSPHERE
          STRENGTH)

Figure 7

delightfully simple. We knew at once that we had the answer. We
knew it was an important discovery. We were elated beyond description. It did not matter that we had been on the verge of
taking the simple step for months and had somehow failed to do
so. It only mattered that we had found something new and important that no one had recognized previously (see Chapter 1).
Our elation was reinforced almost immediately by a burst of
enthusiasm for investigating the additional meaning of the simple but elegant concept that had appeared on that blackboard.

The additional meaning began to become evident almost immediately, but the process evolved gradually and it was weeks,
months, and years before other key points were revealed. On the
one hand it was necessary to return to the observations to discover what new information they offered once the context of the
downgoing slab was in place. The data showed, for example, that
the slab had a slightly higher velocity for both compressional and
shear waves than its surroundings did. A quantitative estimate
of the attenuation was measured and the thickness and spatial
extent of the slab were determined. Focal mechanisms provided
important information on the dynamics and the deformation of
the slab. And so on. Interpreting the observations in the new
context (one might call it a paradigm of modest scale on lithospheric plate interaction) became a major activity that produced
results in great variety. That process, in fact, continues today
although at a much lower and diminishing pace.

On the other hand, there was the important task of relating

the new model of the downgoing slab to other parts of earth science. The ferment based on concepts such as continental drift and sea floor spreading was growing rapidly, and the new information on the downgoing slab and other developments added to the excitement. It was a time for seeing each new contribution in the overall context of earth dynamics, an exciting and a stimulating time indeed.

For example, our seismic data from Tonga-Fiji revealed the seismic properties (velocity and attenuation) of the mantle of that region. The spatial distribution of those properties led to a model whose configuration suggested a behavior based on rheological properties such as strength and viscosity. We were thus stimulated to bring the well-known rheological concepts of lithosphere and asthenosphere into interpretation of the seismic data and so into the evolving story of plate tectonics (figures 7 and 8). The crust-mantle classification scheme of seismology and the lithosphere-asthenosphere scheme of rheology were brought together—finally. The dichotomy was resolved and the two parts fell into place so neatly and accurately as to inspire confidence in the observations and methods of scientists of an earlier era, even though they had not been able to produce the unified scheme.

Integrating the lithosphere into the seismological world was a relatively easy step for geophysicists, for the subject matter all fell within the realm of geophysics. The dynamics of the downgoing slab forced us into less familiar realms as well. One was petrology. The arcs were well known as sites of major volcanism. Could the volcanism and petrology of rocks of island arcs be fitted into the downgoing slab model, or was there evidence from petrology that could be used to show the model was impossible? We searched the literature, finding nothing to support or deny the model, at least without intense reinterpretation of the data, until we came to an innovative paper published in 1962 by Robert Coats. Coats's hypothesis to explain the volcanic petrology of the Aleutian arc was based on underthrusting of surface materials to depths of about 100 km and matched well with our story of the slab of lithosphere descending to still greater depths. Coats's paper had not received much attention before that time, but once its place in the plate model was recognized, it became widely known. It was an example of an innovative and daring contribution (see Chapter 2) brushed aside temporarily by those bound by the chains of convention.

Other geophysicists, using seismic reflection data, had found extensional grabens on the outer wall of the deep trenches. At first this evidence for extension seemed to conflict with the notion that compression would result as the slab descended and two plates converged, but we quickly recognized that bending of the slab could produce extension near the outer surface of the bend even though the bulk of the plate was not in tension, and that explanation became, and remains, widely accepted.

In essence what we were finding was that our discovery was important because many kinds of data, previously thought to be unrelated, fit and fell together under the new model (see Chapter 6). And the story grew stronger and better as new and different kinds of data fell into place.

We also sought confirmation of our Tonga-Fiji observations for other similar structures, i.e., arcs with associated deep earthquakes elsewhere in the world. There were limited relevant observations, except in the case of Japan, where to our surprise we found that Japanese seismologists Utsu and Katsumata had published studies showing that the deep seismic zone in Japan is indeed also a zone of low attenuation. They had not, however, related that zone to the emerging global tectonics story or to the lithosphere in Japan or elsewhere, and so the significance of their results to tectonics initially went unappreciated. It was also surprising, and comforting, to learn that the propagation of the seismic waves in the zone of low attenuation was so efficient that deep earthquakes in Japan were felt by humans where the inclined zone reached the surface and not felt by humans immediately over and closer to the same earthquake hypocenter! The effect was clearly not a subtle one, another sign that the observations were robust and that we were on the right track (see Chapter 6).

Partly as a result of our study, current thinking about the dynamics of motion in the mantle changed to include the notion of thin plates that moved about on the surface. Previously those leaders, such as Holmes and Hess, who had with great foresight postulated convective motion in the mantle with upwelling at the ridges and descending currents at the arcs, had not incorporated the concept of surficial plates in that convection pattern, even though the concepts of lithosphere and asthenosphere were already known in other circles. In our first paper on this subject we drew attention to the concept of mobility of a lithosphere that covers large parts of the earth's surface and is discontinuous. It was, so far as I know, the first incorporation of the concept of the lithosphere and lithospheric units into the stream of development of what would become plate tectonics. We did not, however, determine the spatial pattern or the dynamic global pattern of the plates. In earlier eras, some geologists, such as Daly and Wilson, had ideas about the role of a strong surface layer in earth dynamics, but those ideas somehow did not catch on as they might have.

At about the time Isacks and I were making the discovery and recognizing the importance of the mobile lithosphere, Elsasser, at Maryland and Princeton, on the basis of on physical reasoning, developed some similar notions on earth dynamics that incorporated a strong mobile outer layer. He called that layer the tectosphere, but it was essentially equivalent to the lithosphere. We learned of each other's results during a visit by Elsasser to Lamont just a few days before our paper was presented at the famous spring AGU meeting in 1967. At that same meeting, Jason Morgan, also of Princeton, presented the first paper on the geographical plan of the major plates, a half dozen in number, and he used Euler's theorem for motion of rigid caps on a sphere to describe the plate motion.

Later, McKenzie and Parker, referencing our paper but in a narrow context, advanced the subject by showing that focal mechanisms over a large area of the Pacific were consistent with motion of a plate. Shortly thereafter, Bryan Isacks, Lynn Sykes and I joined forces to write a comprehensive paper on seismology and global tectonics. A part of that paper integrated the discovery into seismology and geodynamics in a fairly complete manner. A block diagram in that paper illustrated the elements of plate tectonics, including subduction, in a simple fashion (figure 8); it helped to spread the concept widely at a time when plate tectonics was becoming the new paradigm. The comprehensive paper by the three of us became far more well known than the first report on the downgoing slab and was a very satisfying achievement, but for me the thrill of discovery was clearly greater in that first effort.

The discovery spawned a series of succeeding studies too numerous and diverse to elucidate here. Isacks, with Molnar, Barazangi, and others, continued to develop the study of deep earthquakes as they relate to the dynamics of the island arcs. The

Seismology and New Global Tectonics

·Figure 8

subject has been a remarkably fertile one and a prime source of our understanding of mantle geodynamics.

At present the discovery has long since faded into obscurity as a separate entity, but the discovered features continue to be an integral part of the concept of plate tectonics, and particularly the component of that concept that is the subduction process. In terms of geologic consequences this process is one of, if not the, most important in the earth.

In retrospect, it seems clear that the discovery related in this case history was a product of many factors. One, surely, was good fortune. Fate, and not carefully considered, conscious decision, brought the participants together and into positions where the discovery could happen to us. Fate put us in touch with various pieces of information that would later blend together to produce the discovery. But in addition to that strong dose of good fortune, there was also a component of good judgment, hard work, and sound strategy that was critical to the discovery. Indeed, following certain of the guidelines of this book often resulted in decisions that turned out to be correct and critical in retrospect.

For example, the decision to go into the field and make new observations of a previously poorly observed yet obviously important phenomenon, deep earthquakes, was a sound and key decision. To do so in the absence of a well-specified model for testing according to the tradition of the "scientific method" was also an important move. Keeping alert for significance of the results outside as well as within the specialty was important. And so were many of the other attitudes and strategies found in the guidelines of this book and referred to in the preceding paragraphs. Adhering to those guidelines resulted in the proper decision so often that the discovery occurred. Was the discovery made at the earliest that it could have been made? Likely it was not. But it is clear that the discovery was made before others following different paths or strategies were in a position to make it. The path may not have been the best possible, but it was better than all those followed by others (see Chapter 2).

It is also clear that this particular discovery, like many or perhaps all discoveries, did not require the qualities of a unique individual, a so-called scientific genius. All work in science requires a certain amount of appropriate God-given talent, of course. Science is not for everyone. But there are many individuals who have the talent for scientific discovery and who can make a significant discovery if they maneuver properly within the scientific world so as to take advantage of their opportunities.

If Isacks and I had not found the downgoing slab in 1966–1967, surely some other scientist would have done so within a relatively short time. Scientific discovery, as someone has said, is the revealing of something waiting to be revealed. To make a scientific discovery is not the same as to compose a beautiful piece of music. If the composer had not lived, the piece of music would probably never have been written. If a particular scientist had not lived, his discoveries almost surely would be made a little later by someone else. To keep the science vital, scientists must strive continually to be the first to achieve, but failure to make a particular discovery merely postpones that discovery for an indefinite time. Our achievement was important, useful, and rewarding, but there is nothing about the discovery or the discoverers that is so uncommon as to suggest that similar discoveries cannot be made readily by others following a comparable course. Nor does there appear to be any reason why the process of discovery in any science cannot be accelerated by increased effort, increased observation and study, and enhanced understanding and application of the discovery process. We can strive to improve scientific productivity as we do in the case of industrial productivity.

Finally, for those who are interested in the thoughts that pass through the heads of scientists during a period of discovery, I would like to relate the incident of the sinking paper towel.

The first model of the lithospheric plate at a subduction zone, the same model in use today, requires that the plate, which is nearly flat beneath undisturbed sea floor, bend rather abruptly as it enters the subduction zone, then flatten again as it descends into the asthenosphere at the appropriate angle of dip. We recognized, shortly after the model was formulated, that this behavior was required by the plate, but we were puzzled about why the slab should straighten out again once it had been curved. Why, in other words, did it not continue to bend or at least remain in the curved state?

We finally guessed that some sort of hydrodynamic behavior must be involved, and I now believe that is the correct explanation. At the time, however, we were busy and excited and had no time to investigate this matter thoroughly. We sought a quick test to determine the validity of the idea. In haste we filled a nearby sink, floated a paper towel on the surface of the water, forced the end of the towel under water, and then released the system. To our delight the submerged portion pulled the rest of the towel down into the water. And the towel descended by moving horizontally to a particular point, then bending as it moved around the curve, and then, wondrously, flattening as it descended farther. The paper towel did just what we had hypothesized the lithospheric slab had done. The analogy (see Chapter 2) supported our intuition, and we moved beyond that problem to other topics.

I cannot defend this procedure or this experiment on purely scientific grounds. The paper towel in water was not necessarily a good analogy or scale model for the slab. Another brand of paper towel might well have behaved differently. Anyone could easily criticize this experiment as it was conceived and carried out. Nevertheless, it was a factor in the way in which our thinking proceeded, and it enabled us to move beyond an obstacle and consider other data which, it turned out, did indeed provide substantial validity for the model. Our test was not a sound one scientifically, but it was a factor in the way and the rate at which science progressed (see Chapter 2).

Closing Remarks

W E near the point at which the reader and the writer will, figuratively, part company. It is my hope that this book has provided a stimulating and profitable experience, particularly for those entering or near the beginning of a scientific career. I have tried to convey a set of attitudes and procedures that have enhanced serendipity in the past. My conviction is that at least some will continue to do so in the future. I await eagerly the report of some young scientist who has profited from this book. I also look forward to comments, positive or negative, from seasoned discoverers who have the same or different thoughts. If a prolonged discourse on this subject begins and results in better understanding of the phenomenon of discovery, so much the better.

It may be worthwhile in this concluding section to draw attention again to a few themes that have appeared in previous pages in one form or another.

One continuing theme is that the essence of science is merely the collecting and organizing of observations. The collecting of comprehensive observations is a huge, difficult, and almost overwhelming task, of course. And the organizing of those observations is a formidable challenge to the most talented theoretical scientists of our time. But the essence of the task remains simple. This characterization of science, which is, of course, held by others as well, is nevertheless a somewhat different and less lofty description of science than some would have.

The point of the book is not, however, to raise a debate on the philosophy of science. It is to use this view of science as a basis for maneuvering into a position favorable for discovery. The strategy is to put oneself into close association with new and significant observations. That is the most favorable position for a would-be discoverer. The strategy is obvious for those who recognize that sound observations are the ultimate truth, the only truth, of science.

Seeing science in this light also conveys an appropriate view of the structure of science apart from observation. The structure is, in a sense, always a fictitious one generated in, and existing in, the minds of humans. It is an ingeniously concocted, complicated web of interlocking laws, theories, doctrines, and hypotheses, each of which must be held subject to change if observations so demand. The theoretical side of science is something like a historical novel that holds true to the facts where the facts are known and then weaves an interesting story to fill the gaps. But unlike the novel, by the rules of science, science must be altered as tests of the story against observation dictate.

The emphasis on observation opens special avenues to discovery. Discoveries, it seems, can be forced to occur in the future, as they often have in the past, by the deliberate making of observations of new phenomena or new frontiers. To produce a major discovery we need not wait for the birth of a genius. We need only to recognize an important unexplored frontier and then plan and carry out a sound program of observation of that frontier. Experience tells us that once the observations are in hand and appropriately distributed, some inspired mind will devise a clever theoretical way to organize the observations, but that mind would not make that discovery in the absence of the data.

The critical dependence of science on observation tells us of the limitations on scientific discovery. Once all of the observations that can be made of a particular subject and other relevant objects are made and those observations all fall into a satisfactory scheme of organization, the discovery phase of that part of science is complete. Nothing better can be done in the absence of additional relevant observations. With an entire universe remaining to be observed in detail, this conclusion hardly spells the death knell of science, but certain branches of nature that are isolated from other branches may already be beyond the discovery phase.

A second theme that weaves through the preceding sections concerns the need for the would-be discoverer to see his or her efforts from a variety of perspectives different from those of the typical research specialist in that field. It is valuable to be able to view one's work from the perspective of colleagues, from the perspective of scientists in other fields, from the perspective of the part of society that supports the scientist's efforts, and from the perspective of the uninitiated in science.

Third, this book is intended as a positive contribution; i.e., it is designed to encourage those who would do the "right" thing for science and for society. It is intended to be upbeat and to leave the reader with a more optimistic outlook on the chances of making a major discovery. Furthermore, it encourages the reader to act in a responsible and respectable manner while practicing science in pursuit of discovery. I have implicitly assumed that all motivations are honorable and all activities are carried out with honor and integrity.

Having spent a career spanning nearly half a century in science, I am not so naive as to believe that science, or any activity of humans, is always carried out in that fashion. A skeptic, or what I have referred to as a "scowl and scoffer," may claim this book is unrealistic because it omits mention of some of the less desirable characteristics of some scientists, even though such scientists may be few. A quote from J. Ziman (1957) is illustrative.

> It is refreshing to be reminded that eccentricity and anarchy, serendipity and obsession, counter-suggestion, jealousy, paranoic suspicion, spasmodic laziness, arrogant virtuosity, and other individualistic traits are still to be regarded as essential ingredients in scientific creation.

Of course, there is some truth in that statement by Ziman. Science has its share, perhaps more than its share, of magnificent or overpowering egos and the behavior that accompanies them. But the statement begs the question of whether it must always be that way in science. I would say that it need not. A great deal of important scientific work has been accomplished not only by those whose egos are sufferable but also by those whose personalities are pleasant and considerate. Most scientists are that way. And their behavior is marked by the highest integrity. The guidelines of this book are directed toward those cut in, or striving for, that mold.

As a general question, one might ask whether science is evolving from an early stage, when motivation based on the less appealing ingredients of Ziman's paragraph was a critical element, to a later stage when the processes of doing science are better understood and hence can be carried out entirely by those well adjusted to society. That may, however, be wishful thinking. Some eccentrics, loved or unloved, may always be part of science. In any case we must leave the matter for the future to resolve. In the meantime, those prospective scientists who lack paranoia, arrogance, eccentricity, and the tendency to anarchism that Ziman describes need not feel left out! There is much that can be accomplished by those who lack those particular qualities.

Honesty compels me to make one additional point. I have not shared fully with readers some opportunities for discovery in my field, earth science, that are apparent to me based on application of certain of the guidelines described here. There must be such opportunities, of course. Earth science is full of vitality. There is surely much left to discover. But pinpointing those opportunities is a task and a decision best left to the discoverer. I have not reported all my selections for several reasons. First, and all books and guidelines to the contrary, discovery remains a chancy business. My selections may be wrong and hence misleading. Second, choosing a subject that appears ripe for discovery usually includes the implication that those currently working in that subject are misdirected. It is not fair to those who may be the subject of attack to make that attack without the full documentation that would be out of place in this book. A scientist must expect criticism, is expected to be critical, has the right to defend against the criticism, and also has the right to know the basis for the criticism. Third, and this may be the last of the guidelines, it is not, of course, always prudent to announce an opportunity for discovery before taking the steps necessary to exploit it. There is no reason for an individual to generate a rabble of competitors at an earlier time than necessary. I would like to exploit the opportunities that I see before the crowd does so!

Let me draw attention again to a point made in the introduction. What I have described here is a style, but not the only style, for discovery. Others may have and may choose other styles. If so, and if they are successful, I hope they will take the trouble to add them to the literature on this subject.

Finally, if nothing else, I hope this book draws some attention to the art of discovery and to the paucity of literature on the subject, particularly literature directed to the prospective scientist. Scientific journals overflow the shelves of the libraries today, but few of them address, or tolerate discussion of, the subjective side of discovery. There is a professionalized literature on this subject by behavioral scientists, or science historians, or philosophers of science. I do not wish to be critical of this literature or the scholarly efforts that have gone into it. It is, however, directed largely to scholars in those fields. Such literature is not widely read by most active scientists and, in any case, it is not usually designed to provide guidance based on past experience to the active scientist. There is a need, in other words, for development of a subject that one might term *applied* history of science or "applied" philosophy of science. There seems no reason why this topic should not be more widely taught in class, written in books and other scientific literature for scientists, and discussed in special sessions at meetings of scientific societies.

Postscript

As noted earlier, and as is surely evident to the reader who has persevered to this point, this volume is an exposition of my views on certain aspects of science, and particularly on some ways to discover in science. Those views have been arrived at almost completely independently of library research designed to ascertain the views of others on this subject. I have read some of the literature of philosophy of science and history of science, of course, but the views I express here are almost entirely a product of my experience and of my personal or professional interaction with other scientists who have passed on their own views and so influenced me. So far as I know, those scientists are not particularly scholars of the art of discovery per se, although, of course, most of them are students of the subject in a practical way because of its relevance to their own principal goal, that is, discovery as opposed to understanding the art of discovery. I make this point at some length to emphasize the independent nature of generation of the guidelines of this book. Some readers may, as I shall do in a moment, wish to compare my guidelines with similar principles generated by others at other times and in other fields. It is important to do so. If indeed investigation shows that the same principles recur and are rediscovered over and over again by scientists discovering in a variety of fields, then the basic premise of this book, that repeatable patterns occur often in the process of discovery, will be strongly reinforced.

In any case, I intend, of course, no claim of priority for the principles and ideas expressed here. Although I have arrived at them more or less independently, nevertheless it is my conviction that most if not all have surely recurred often in the long history of science, sometimes passing from one scientist to the next, sometimes appearing afresh in the mind of a scientist who gains experience with the workings of science. If this book has value, it may be because (1) these principles are assembled conveniently in one place, (2) the principles illustrate a set of convictions of one single scientist, and (3) the examples are taken from earth science, a field that commonly receives little emphasis in modern books on the workings of science.

In this latter connection, and because the comparison brings out some points that I think strengthen the case that is central to this work, I would like to draw attention to a recent book entitled *Discovering* by Robert Scott Root-Bernstein (Harvard University Press, 1989). Root-Bernstein's book came to my attention only after my own book was submitted for publication, and so, except for these few paragraphs, it had no influence on my writing. The two books, in other words, were conceived and written completely independently of one another.

Although the titles are somewhat similar, the books are not. Root-Bernstein's book is a scholarly work, a consequence of years of literature research on the subject of scientific discoveries and discoverers. My book is largely based on one individual's experiences in active research. Root-Bernstein presents a lengthy list of references on the subject. I present only a few. The style of his book is also much different from that of mine. It is fictional and the setting is a roundtable discussion or seminar involving a group of scientists and students of the scientific process. This format allows the author to expose a wide variety of views on a particular topic, and often it is not obvious which view the author might prefer. My book states my views with conviction and makes little attempt to present views that others might have.

In Root-Bernstein's book, the examples of discovery are taken largely from physics, biology, and chemistry with only an occasional reference to geology. The examples of my book are largely from geology, including geophysics, with an occasional reference to physics.

Nevertheless, in spite of the very pronounced differences in style, format, length, sources, and examples, there are certain obvious parallels between Root-Bernstein's book and mine. Both are based on in the conviction that the doing of science could be enhanced through improved understanding of the scientific process and appropriate feedback of that knowledge into scientific research of the future. Both authors claim the same purpose, i.e., to stimulate at least one (but preferably more, of course) young scientist to bigger and better discovery.

Near the end of Root-Bernstein's book, one of the fictional characters, in a form of summary, presents a manual of strategies for discovering. The sources of the strategies are diverse. Often the points of strategy are associated with, or drawn from, a scientific giant or authority of the past. Although the correspondence is not one for one, I was pleased to find a rather close correspondence between many of those strategies and mine, particularly since mine come almost entirely from experience in the field of earth science and virtually all of Root-Bernstein's strategies come from other fields of science. The point could not be more clear. Certain aspects of the process of discovery are often repeated from one discovery to the next and without regard to the particular scientific field. Such a clear demonstration of this point strengthens the view that some aspects of the discovery process can be taught and the scientific enterprise enhanced in so doing. Needless to say, I was very pleased to find such agreement and so many specific points of agreement.

There are some clear-cut differences as well, of course. I give only two examples here but there are others. The use of Occam's razor is not challenged in Root-Bernstein's book as I have challenged it. Nor do I support a literal interpretation of what Root-Bernstein calls Maier's law, i.e., "If the data don't fit the theory, ignore the data." In other cases, Root-Bernstein's style of exposing many viewpoints on an issue without taking a stand in favor of one does not permit direct comparison.

In any case, the principal message of this comparison seems clear. Discoverers in science again and again follow similar paths of reasoning, activity, and behavior, and this observation validates the concept of setting up certain principles or guidelines to aid potential discoverers of the future.

References

Allegre, C. 1988. *The Behavior of the Earth* (English translation). Cambridge, Mass.: Harvard University Press.

Beveridge, W. I. B. 1957. *The Art of Scientific Investigation.* New York: Vintage Books.

Coulomb, J. 1972. *Sea Floor Spreading and Continental Drift.* Dordrecht, Holland: Reidel.

Holton, G. 1978. *The Scientific Imagination: Case Studies.* Cambridge, England: Cambridge University Press.

Isacks, B., J. Oliver, and L. Sykes. 1968. "Seismology and the New Global Tectonics." *Journal of Geophysical Research,* 73(18): 5855–5899.

Kuhn, T. S. 1962. *The Structure of Scientific Revolutions.* Chicago: University of Chicago Press.

Marvin, U. B. 1973. *Continental Drift.* Washington, D.C.: Smithsonian Institution Press.

Menard, H. W. 1986. *The Ocean of Truth.* Princeton, N.J.: Princeton University Press.

Oliver, J. and B. Isacks. 1967. "Deep Earthquake Zones, Anomalous Structures in the Upper Mantle, and the Lithosphere." *Journal of Geophysical Research,* 72(16): 4259–4275.

Root-Bernstein, R. S. 1989. *Discovering.* Cambridge, Mass.: Harvard University Press.

Ziman, J. 1957. "Minerva 9:456." In G. Y. Craig and E. J. Jones, eds. 1985. *A Geological Miscellany.* Princeton, N.J.: Princeton University Press.

Index

Academic freedom, 166
Activity change, as result of discovery, 161-62
Adaptation of techniques, 66-68
Age: of continents, 22; of crustal rocks, 112; of earth, 46; of scientist and discovery, 128, 156-58; of sea floor, 22
Aleutian arc, volcanic petrology, 181
Allegre, C., 27
Analogy, 57-59, 186
Antarctica, scientific exploration, 114
Arcs, physiographic, 168
Arctic studies, 101-2
Art: of discovery, 142; science and, 9-10; of winning, 54-56
Asthenosphere, 107, 170, 181, 182

Atmospheric energy, and seismic waves, 95
Atoms, 158
Attitudes for discovery, 97-126
Audacity, 113-14
Audience for this book, 11-12

Barazangi, Muawia, 44, 183
Barrell, Joseph, 170
Behavior of scientists, 189-90
Belts of seismicity, 44-45, 70
Big science, 149-52
Bird, J. M., 23
Body waves, 75
Boldness in research design, 113-14
Boorstin, Daniel J., 153
Brainstorming sessions, 51
Brown, Paul, 83-84
Bucher, Walter, 34, 108-10
Bullard, Edward, 19, 20, 34, 114

Bureaucracy, and science, 152-54

Buried continental crust, 25-26, 39, 47, 64-65

Careers in science, 100

Cartographers, 147-48

Case history of discovery, 167-86

Challenges, pleasure in, 100-2

Chamberlain, R. T., 170

Change: in activity, as result of discovery, 161-62; and discovery, 46; patterns of, 94; in science, 104-7

Characteristics: of innovators, 125-26; for success, 97

Childlike thinking, 122-23

Choices: of deep drilling sites, 112-13; of deep earthquake study site, 174; of graduate school, 81-84, 169; of study project, 89-91, 172

Citations, 56, 162

Classification, 31, 133-34, 170; crust-mantle, 181

Clever research papers, 161

Coats, Robert, 181

COCORP (Consortium for Continental Reflection Profiling), 25, 38-39

Columbus, Christopher, 37, 63

Committee activities, 51

Communication, jargon and, 71-72

Competition, 54-56, 110

Computers, 148

Concepts, scientific, 104-5; understanding of, 98-100

Consortium for Continental Reflection Profiling (CO-CORP), 25, 38-39

Continental crust, buried, 25-26, 39, 47, 64-65; lower boundary, 80-81

Continental drift, 17-18, 20-21, 33, 98, 128; Bucher-King debate, 109-10; Jef-freys and, 73-75; Taylor and, 85

Continental geology, 25

Continents, 46, 58, 65; age of, 22

Contraction theory, 16

Convection, 58, 107, 182

Conventional wisdom, discovery and, 52

Convergent zones, 168

Core of earth, 76-77

Coulomb, J., 27

Cox, Allan, 20, 38, 157

Crary, Albert, 101-2

Cream-skimming, 69-71

Creativity, 4, 121

Credit for work, 110

Cretaceous-Tertiary boundary, 26

Criticism, 190

Crowd-following, 32-34

Crustal rocks, ages of, 112

Crust-mantle boundary, 134

Crystalline basement, deep drilling of, 111-13

Curve of discovery, 92-93

Dalrymple, Brent, 20, 38

Daly, Reginald, 106-7, 170

Dangers of success, 155-56

Darwin, Charles, 37-38

Data, unrelated, discoveries and, 182

Data collection, see Observations, scientific

Dedication to science, 101-2

Deep drilling, 111-13

Deep earthquakes, 45, 172-85

Deep mine, observatory in, 171

Deep sea trenches, 58; gravity anomalies, 114, 130-31

Deformation: of earth, 106-7, 132; of rocks, 15-16

The Deformation of the Earth's Crust, Bucher, 108-9

Democracy, discovery and, 165-66

Detailed step-by-step exploration, 62-65

Dewey, John, 23, 157

Directions, new, for research, 33-34

Discoverers, 146-49

Discovering, Root-Bernstein, 194-95

Discovery, 1-5, 185; art of, 10; attitudes and personal traits, 97-126; case history, 167-86; curve of, 92-93; democracy and, 165-66; emotions of, 7; future of, 26-27, 188-89; guidelines for, 5, 11-13, 28, 184-85; important, to recognize, 160-64; limits to, 140-42; literature of, 191, 194-95; methods, 24-25; organizational structure of science and, 149-52; principles of, 193-94; society and, 8-9; strategies for, 31-65, 195; tactics for, 66-96

Doell, Richard Rayman, 20, 38

Do-it-righters, 146-49

Dorman, H. James, 44

Downgoing slab model, 180-81

Drake, Charles, 82

Dreaming, 121-22

Earth: deformation of, 106-7, 132; exploration of, 47, 92, 141; incorrect assumptions about, 173; interior of, 76-77, 170

The Earth, Jeffreys, 74-75

Earth science, 5-6, 41, 160, 190; adaptation of technology, 67; age of discoverers, 128, 156-58; changes in, 46; exploration, 62; geologic maps, 78; history, 13-30; and intuition, 50; observations, 72-78; sophisticated procedures, 99; specialization, 144-45

Earthquake focal mechanisms, 88-89

Earthquake-generated waterborne sound, 169-70

Earthquakes, study of, 95

Earthquake seismology, 44-45, 75-78

Education, scientific, 122; funding of, 118-19

Edwards, Dick, xi

Einstein, Albert, 50, 123

Elastic phenomena, 170

Elitism of science, 165

Elsasser, Walter, 157, 183

Emotions of discovery, 7

Empiricism of science, 137-38

Enthusiasm, 108-10

Epicenters, global maps, 44-45

Era of science, 139

Eureka phenomenon, 179

Evaluation, in science, 10; of discoveries by others, 160-62; of discoveries by self, 163-64; of scientific projects, 151-52

Ewing, Maurice, xi-xii, 19, 20, 34, 38, 50, 53-54, 70, 148, 169-70; as teacher, 82

Experience of discovery, 4-5

Experimental physics, 86
Experiments, scientific, 137
Exploration, geographical, 14, 47, 62-65, 92, 141, 147; Antarctic, 114; data from, 69; of new frontiers, 37-39
Extraterrestrial bodies, impact of, 26

Failure of hypotheses, 34, 60
False claims, 116
Fate, ix, 184; control of, 38; and discovery, 34, 125
Faulting, postglacial, 131
Field, Richard, 34
Field geologists, 81
First, importance of being, 55-56
Fixist theories, 15-16
Flux-gate magnetometers, 67-68
Focal mechanisms of earthquakes, 88-89
Frontiers of science, 24-25; new, exploration of, 37-39, 62-65; observation of, 188
Funding of science, 19, 118-20, 145, 149-52, 174; public, 152-54; and specialization, 143
Future of science, 26-27, 139-40

Geographical exploration, 14, 47, 92, 141, 147
Geography, 13-14
Geological exploration, 47
Geologic maps, 78
Geology, 13-14, 41, 158-60; discoveries in, 27, 141-42; future of, 27; global, 65
Geomagnetism, 170

Global rift system, 70
Global seismicity, 44-45, 56
Global tectonics theories, 16-20
Goals of science, 53-54, 98, 99; focus on, 40
Goals of scientists, 5; discovery as, 7
Good fortune, 125, 184
Government funding of science, 19, 152-54; science advisory committees, 166
Graduate school, choice of, 81-84, 169
Gravity anomalies in deep sea trenches, 114, 130-31
Gravity field measurements, 114
Griggs, David, 107
Guidelines for discovery, 5, 11-13, 28, 184-85, 190; personal traits and attitudes, 97-126; recognition of important discoveries, 160-64; strategies, 31-65; tactics, 66-96; warnings, 127-34

Hard work, 124-25
Haskell, Norman, 148
Heezen, Bruce, 20, 69-70
Hess, Harry, 21, 37, 156
High-frequency seismic waves, 169-71, 179
History, 28; of discovery, 3-4; of earth science, 13-30; of science, applied, 191
Holmes, Arthur, 107
Honors, 155
Hot streaks, 50-51
Human factors in science, 42-43
Humility, 110-13
Hypotheses, 60-61, 104-5,

137; testing of, 49; unconventional, 60-61

Imaginative hypotheses, 60-61
Important discoveries, to recognize, 160-64
Improvisation, to achieve goals, 54
Incorrect assumptions: about deep earthquakes, 172-73; about ocean basins, 20
Independence, discovery and, 32-34
Indoctrination, 127-29
Inner core of earth, 76-77
Innovation, 4, 11-12
Innovators, 35-36, 121-22, 125-26
Instruments for discovery, 66-68
Interdisciplinary studies, jargon and, 117
Interior of earth, 25, 26, 47, 76-77, 170; convection in, 58; incorrect assumptions about, 173
International treaties, 172
Intuition, 48-52, 173; analogy and, 57
Iridium anomaly, 26
Irving, T., 20
Isacks, Bryan, 22, 44, 172, 173-86
Island arcs, 22-23, 56, 58, 130-31, 181; deep earthquakes and, 172-84

Japan, seismological studies, 182
Jargon, 71-72, 116-17; and specialization, 143
Jeffreys, Harold, 73-75
Journals, scientific, 143
Joy of discovery, 7

Katsumata, M. 182
Kelvin, Lord William Thompson, 16, 129
King, Lester, 10
Knowledge of subject, 110-11
Kola Peninsula, deep hole, 113
Kuhn, T. S., 24
Kusch, Polykarp, x

Lamont-Doherty Geological Observatory, 109, 169-71; and sea floor spreading, 178
Large projects, 145-46, 149-52; leaders of, 156
Laws, scientific, 104-5; Bucher's, 108-9
Leadership: pressures of, 156; by teachers, 83-84
Learning by doing, 86-87
LeGrand, H. E., 28
Lehmann, Inge, 77
LePichon, Xavier, 23
Life style of scientists, 101-2
Limits of discovery, 188-89
Literature: of discovery, 191, 194-95; scientific, search of, 84-86
Lithosphere, 170, 181; mobility of, 182-83; subduction, 168-86
Little science, 149-52
Long duration seismic waves, 148
Long-term view of science, 46-48
Low attenuation zone, seismic waves and, 182
Low-frequency seismology, 171
Lunatic fringe, 61

McKenzie, D., 183
Magnetic anomalies, 20, 21, 68, 178; spatial pattern, 79

Maier's law, 195
Mainstream, departure from, 32-34, 171
Mantle: incorrect assumptions about, 173; motion in, 182-83; seismic properties, 181
Mapmaking, 147-48
Mapping, geological, 47
Marine magnetic anamolies, 68, 79
Marvin, U.B., 27
Mass spectrometers, 67
Matthews, D. H., 21, 91, 155
Measurement techniques, adaptation of, 66
Menard, H. W., *Ocean of Truth*, 27-28
Metasediments, 134
Microseisms, 95
Mid-Atlantic Ridge, 75
Migmatites, 134
Millikan, Robert Andrews, 50
Mine, observatory in, 171
Mineralogy, 79-80
Minimum Astonishment Principle, 51-52
Mobilist theories, 16-18
Models, 159-60; quantitative, 78
Moho, 80-81, 134
Molnar, Peter, 183
Moon, seismograph on, 171
Morgan, Jason, 23, 98-99, 157, 183
Morley, L., 21, 155
Mountain formation, 107, 159

National Science Foundation (NSF), 174
Neptunists, 40, 72
New directions for research, 33-34, 56, 171
New frontiers, exploration of, 37-39

New observations, 61, 188; discovery and, 146, 174
New perspectives on science, 87-89
News reports of discoveries, 162
Nonquestions, 43-45
NSF (National Science Foundation), 174
Nuclear test ban treaty, 172

Objectivity, 59-60; about discoveries, 163
Observations, scientific, 47-48, 49, 60, 103-4, 187-89; and change, 106; discovery and, 38, 163-64; earth science, 72-78; new, 61, 146, 174; organization of, 137-38; skimming of, 69-71; techniques, 67; unexplained, 93, 96; unrelated, discoveries and, 182
Occam's razor, 129-32, 195
Ocean basins, 18; exploration of, 64, 113-14; floors of, 73; studies of, 19-22, 34, 38
Oceanic deep drilling, 112
Ocean of Truth, Menard, 27-28
Ocean trenches, 58; gravity anomalies, 114, 130-31
Older scientists: discoveries by, 156-58; unconventional hypotheses, 61
Opportunity: identification of, 36; new areas of study, 56
Optimism, 108, 115-16
Organizational structure of science, 137-38, 149-52
Originality, 56
Overspecialization, 144
Oxburgh, R., 23

Pacific Basin, 20, 46
Paleomagnetism, 20, 170
Paper towel, sinking, 186
Paradigm discovery, 24-26
Parker, R., 183
Past scientific achievements, respect for, 105-7
Patterns, 78-81
Pekeris, C., 148
Perils of success, 155-56
Personal characteristics of scientists, 42-43; for discovery, 97-126
Perspective on science, 39-41, 46-48, 189; new, 87-89
Pessimism, 115-16
Petrology, 181
Phases in scientific development, 94
Philosophy of science, 136; applied, 191
Physicists, and sports, xi
Physics, 158-59
Planetary science, 63
Plate tectonics, 5-6, 23, 33-34, 56, 58-59, 89, 112, 130-31, 183-84; earthquake seismology and, 44; Jeffreys and, 73-75; and specialization, 144; subduction, 168-86; writings about, 27-28
Politics: negotiatons, 172; and scientific funding, 151
Popper, K., 104
Postglacial faulting, 131
Predictions, scientific, 137-38
Preliminary investigations of study, 90
Press, Frank, 82, 148, 169
Pretense, avoidance of, 116-18
Previously unknown data, discoveries and, 163-64
Principle of Minimum Astonishment, 51-52

Principles of discovery, 193-94
Principles of Physical Geology, Holmes, 107
Problem for study, choice of, 89-91, 172
Process of discovery, 3-4
Professionalism, 72, 116-17
Professors, for graduate study, 81-84, 169
Profiling of continental crust, 25-26, 39
Project, choice of, 89-91, 172
Proof, in science, 104
Public funding for research, 152-54
Publishers, and specialization, 143
Puzzle-solving science, 24, 144, 147-49; and discovery, 110-11

Questions, childlike, 122-23

Reading, peripheral, 84-86
Rebellion against status quo, 35-37
Recognition for discovery, 155
Reconaissance-style exploration, 62-65, 69
Reductionist style of science, 158-59
Research, scientific, xii; and discovery, 146; funding of, 119-20, 145, 174
Respect for scientific achievement, 105-7
Responsibility of scientists, 9, 119-20, 189
Revelle, Roger, 34
Revisions of science, 104
Rewards of scientific success, 100-2, 155
Rift system, 70
Rivalry, 110

Rocks, 14-16; classifications,
134; ages of, 112; magnetic
fields, 20; of ocean crust, 20
Root-Bernstein, Robert Scott,
Discovering, 194-95
Runcorn, Stanley Keith, 20
Rutherford, Ernest, 82-83

Sagan, Carl, 88
San Andreas Fault, 45
San Francisco earthquake
(1906), 45
Scale, change of, 87-88
Science, 5, 41-43, 139; and
art, 9-10; and bureaucracy,
152-54; career demands,
100-2; competition in, 54;
enthusiasm for, 108-10;
limitations on, 143-46; objectivity in, 59-60; observations and, 187-89; perspective on, 39-41, 46-48; progress of, 93-94, 103-4; society
and, 8-9, 118-20; specialization in, 39-41; structure of,
137-38; style of, 24, 146-49,
158-60; success in, ix, 34,
155-56; talent for, 185;
team research, 149-52; and
vision, 61; World War II and,
19
Scientific journals, 4, 191
Scientific literature, search of,
84-86
Scientific method, 61, 137;
and pretense, 116
Scientific research, xii; funding for, 118-20, 145, 174
Scientists, 9, 42-43, 189-90;
choice of graduate school,
81-84, 169; debt to society,
118-20; intuitive, 48-50;
role in society, 151

Sea floor, 18, 19-21, 34, 64,
73; deep drilling, 112; gravity anomalies, 130-31; magnetic anomalies, 68; spread
of, 21-23, 68, 79, 170, 178-
79; trenches, 58, 114, 130-
31
Secondary problems, 53
Sedimentary basins, 25
Sediments, ocean floor, 123
Seismic belts, 44-45, 70
Seismic waves, 76-77, 95,
148, 173-82
Seismographs, 95
Seismology, 75-78, 95, 148;
Lamont-Doherty program,
170-71; and plate tectonics,
44-45
Serendipity, ix, 3, 37-39;
choice of deep drilling sites,
112-13
Shear waves, high-frequency,
170, 171, 179
Significance of problems for
study, 90
Simple explanations, 130-32
Sinking paper towel, 186
Sites: for deep drilling, choice
of, 112; of deep earthquake
activity, 174
Skills, learning of, 86-87
Society: and continental crust
studies, 26; and funding for
research, 145; and future of
science, 139; role of scien-
tists, 151; and scientific discovery, 8-9; scientist's debt
to, 118-20
SOFAR channel, 59
Sophistication, 98-100, 161
Sound waves, in ocean, 59
Space exploration, 114
Spatial patterns, 78-81
Specialization, 39-41, 71, 86-

87, 143-44; bureaucracy and, 153-54

Sports, hot streaks, 51

Status, social, of scientists, 9, 119

Status quo, rebellion against, 35-37

Step-by-step exploration, 62-65, 69

Stewart, J. A., 28

Storms at sea, 95

Strategies for discovery, 31-65, 195

Strike-slips, 45

Structure of science, 137-38, 188

Style of science, 10, 12, 158-60; modification of, 24

Subduction, 23, 130, 183, 186; discovery of, 168-86

Subjectivity in science, 12, 42-43, 49, 60-61

Submarine canyons, 64

Success, ix, 41, 101, 155-56; characteristics for, 97; factors in, 125; motivation for, 54; optimism and, 116

Surface of earth, knowledge of, 14-15

Surface waves, 75-76

Surficial plates, 182

Surficial rocks, 14-16

Surprise, 111, 113

Sykes, Lynn, 22, 44, 170-71, 178, 183-84

Synthesis, 71-72, 94; jargon and, 117

Tactics for discovery, 66-96

Taylor, F. B., 85

Team research, 149-52

Techniques, adaptation of, 66-68

Technology, society and, 8

Tectosphere, 183

Temperature gradient measures, 114

Terminal papers, 93-96

Testing of science, 10, 104-5

Textbook examples, 78

Tharp, Marie, 69-70

Theoretical science, 138

Theories, 104-5

Time, for dreaming, 121

Timing of discovery announcement, 190

Tonga-Fiji deep earthquake project, 174-82

Topic for study, choice of, 89-91, 172

Transcurrent faults, 45

Transform fault hypothesis, 22-23, 36-37, 45, 98-99

Travel times of seismic waves, 173-78

Trivia, avoidance of, 52-54

Turcotte, Donald, 23, 157

Undergraduate programs, 83

Understanding, 98-100

Unexplained observations, 93, 96

Unrelated data, discoveries and, 182

Upper Mantle Project, 171, 174

Utsu, T., 182

Vening Meinesz, F. A., 114

Vine, Fred, 21, 91, 98, 155, 156-57

Visionary hypotheses, 60-61

Volcanic petrology of Aleutian arc, 181

Wallace, A. R., 37-38

Warnings, 127-34

Wave guides, 59, 148, 169-70
Wegener, Alfred, 17-18, 33,
  128, 155, 156
Werner, Abraham Gottlob, 40
Wilson, J. Tuzo, 22, 36-37,
  45, 98, 157, 178
Winning, art of, 54-56

Work, hard, 124-25
World War II, 15, 18-19, 87

Young scientists, 61; discoveries by, 128, 156-58

Ziman, J., 189

"What do we do that leads to discovery?" Jack E. Oliver asks in his thought-provoking book *The Incomplete Guide to the Art of Discovery.* "To discover, act like a discoverer," the author gives this advice to young scientists and science students in his philosophical and inspirational book about scientific discovery and the subjective process that accompanies discovery.

Oliver observed and contributed to major discoveries in the field of solid earth science — plate tectonics and continental drift. Through anecdotes based on the author's own experiences and associations, Oliver leads the reader to recognize how one breaks out of the rut of mundane thinking that traps most of us most of the time. Cartoons by the author further enliven the text.

The Incomplete Guide to the Art of Discovery encourages innovation and discovery by providing insight into the process of discovery, rather than recounting specific discoveries. Scientists and others who seek to develop their capacity to innovate, to create, or to discover must read this book.

JACK E. OLIVER is a geophysicist. He is the Irving Porter Church Professor of Engineering and former chairman of the Department of Geological Sciences at Cornell University where he was also the first director of the Institute for the Study of Continents. He is a member of the National Academy of Sciences and former president of both the Geological Society of America and the Seismological Society of America.